Nikon Z8 Illustrated Guide

A Visual Handbook to Z8 Mastery, from Beginner to Pro

By

Herbert Gunta

Copyright ©2024 Herbert Gunta,

TABLE OF CONTENTS

INTRODUCTION

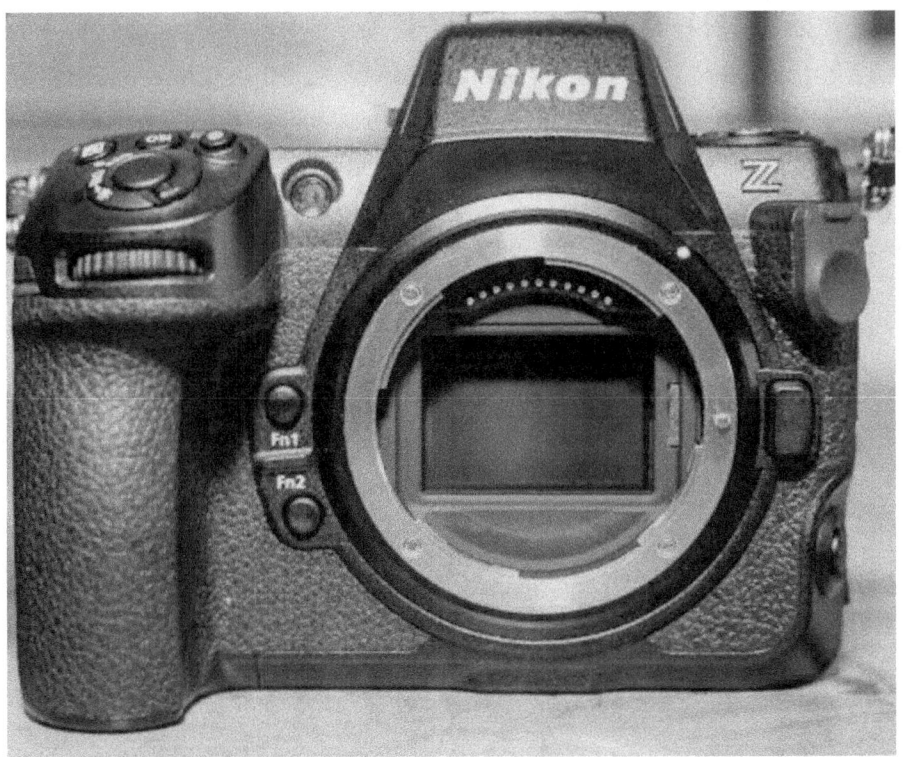

The magnesium alloy body of the Z8 camera emanates an enduring elegance, while the ergonomic handle ensures effortless operation, even for prolonged shooting sessions. The conspicuous dials provide user-friendly controls, encouraging individuals to personalize their experience and explore their photographic prowess. However, the allure of the Z8 transcends mere aesthetics.

Equipped with state-of-the-art technologies, it showcases a 45.7MP layered CMOS sensor that excels at capturing light with remarkable precision and dynamic diversity. When combined with the lightning-fast EXPEED 7 image processor, this formidable sensor unleashes a deluge of creative power. Embrace transient moments with an impressive 120fps rapid filming mode or render landscapes in vivid 8K 24fps video, with every frame showcasing the Z8's unrestrained processing power. Furthermore, the advanced subject and eye-detection autofocus system of the Z8 ensures that your subject is tracked with absolute precision, irrespective of their movements or the illumination conditions. The Z8 achieves steadfast focus locking, guaranteeing flawless pixelation and clarity, whether you're photographing athletes in motion or fauna during a safari. The Z8 transforms videography into a theatrical world; it captures mesmerizing scenes at an immersive resolution of 8K 24fps, or luxuriates in the silky-smooth slow-motion of 4K 120fps, which unveils the concealed beauty within mundane occurrences. By providing unparalleled stability, the Z8's in-body image stabilization further enhances your cinematic vision, even when filming handheld.

Not only is the Z8 a camera, but it also provides access to a thriving ecosystem of Nikon Z lenses. You can explore an extensive assortment of primes, zooms, and specialty lenses, each meticulously designed to maximize the capabilities of the Z8 and accommodate your unique artistic perspective.

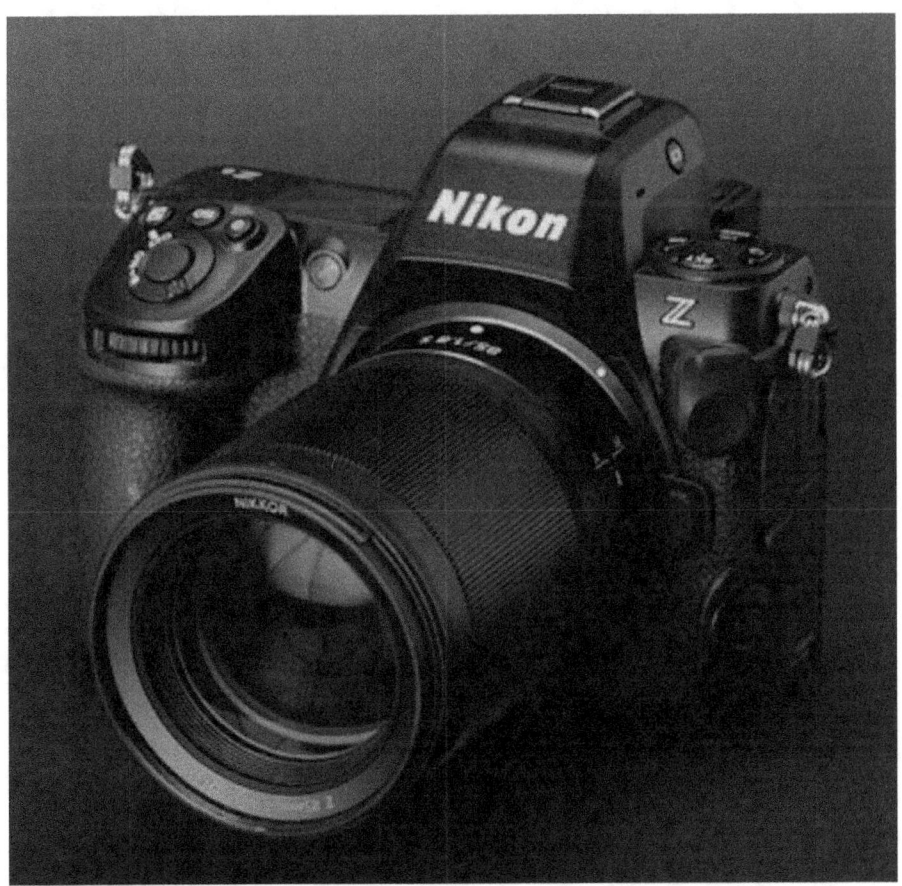

Possession of a Z8 represents not only the acquisition of a camera, but also the formation of a collaborative alliance with a fellow creative. This multifunctional camera encourages you to challenge the limits of your artistic abilities, delve into untraveled photographic domains, and document the world in unprecedented ways. Whether you possess extensive professional experience or are a fervent enthusiast, the Z8 grants you the ability to narrate your own tale, convert transitory instances into enduring recollections, and make a significant impact on the perpetually evolving domain of digital imaging.

7

HOW TO SET UP CAMERA FOR FIRST TIME

The device's initial configuration is quick and straightforward. It requires you to do the following to be properly set up: battery charging, lens attachment, memory card insertion, and clock setting. However, in the event that this is your initial experience with a camera, it is critical that you first acquire proficiency in utilizing the menu button, command dials, and touch screen in order to accurately configure your camera:

Buttons and Controls Required for First Time Setup:

You must first complete a series of tasks prior to using your Z8, the majority of which require the operation of the multi-selection pad and the MENU button.

1. The Menu button: This is situated on the LCD panel's left side. To initiate a menu, simply touch on it. In some instances, pressing it again will terminate a menu or confirm an option before exiting.

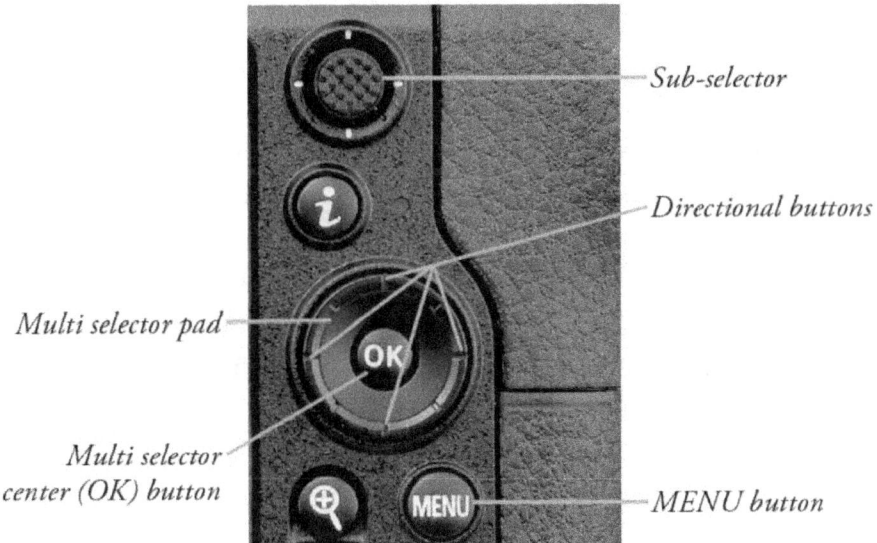

2. The Multi-Selector: This control is analogous to the controls found on a variety of point-and-shoot cameras and other camera models. In addition to a central button, it features thumbpad-sized controls featuring triangle-shaped perspectives at the up, down, left, and right positions. Additionally, it could be pressed diagonally. When browsing through the menus on the LCD monitor or determining one of the 55 user-selectable focus points from the 153 in play, advancing or reversing the display of a sequence of images during picture review, or altering the type of photo details displayed on the screen, the multi selector is frequently employed.

3. The Center of the Multi Selector Button: In conjunction with the right navigation icon, this button facilitates the selection of an object from the menu. The center button can frequently

function as an OK/Enter key, substituting for the "OK" key located on the left side of the camera. However, unlike the OK button, the center button has the capability to be reprogrammed to serve an alternative function under particular circumstances.

4. The "OK" button: To ensure consistency, the enter function should be executed using the OK button instead of the multi selector center button. While it can be utilized in conjunction with other controls during playback (e.g., OK+Up to toggle card locations), its functionalities remain largely unaltered and cannot be reassigned.

5. The Sub-Selector Control: This control, while capable of being modified to navigate menu options, is primarily designed to be a convenient control for setting the focus point. Additionally, it can be squeezed inward to secure focus or exposure.

6. The Main Command and Sub Command dials: They are located in the front and rear of the Z8. The main control dial is employed to alter parameters such as the shutter speed, whereas the sub control dial is utilized to modify an alternative or secondary option. For instance, in Manual exposure mode, the aperture is adjusted via the sub-command dial, whereas the shutter speed is modified via the main command dial. (The dial is only "active" for these adjustments in both instances when the Z8's exposure meter is engaged.) The meter will enter a dormant state after a specified period of time; to

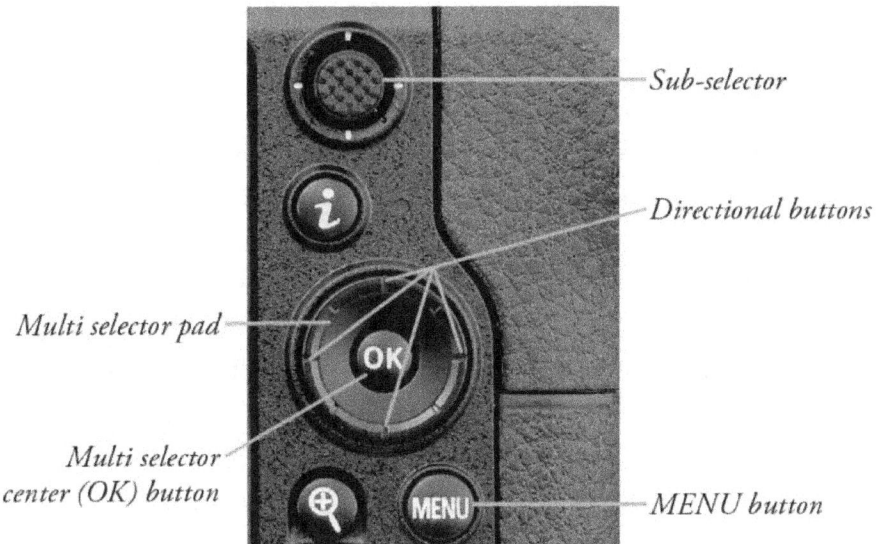

Sub-selector

Directional buttons

Multi selector pad

Multi selector center (OK) button

MENU button

2. The Multi-Selector: This control is analogous to the controls found on a variety of point-and-shoot cameras and other camera models. In addition to a central button, it features thumbpad-sized controls featuring triangle-shaped perspectives at the up, down, left, and right positions. Additionally, it could be pressed diagonally. When browsing through the menus on the LCD monitor or determining one of the 55 user-selectable focus points from the 153 in play, advancing or reversing the display of a sequence of images during picture review, or altering the type of photo details displayed on the screen, the multi selector is frequently employed.

3. The Center of the Multi Selector Button: In conjunction with the right navigation icon, this button facilitates the selection of an object from the menu. The center button can frequently

function as an OK/Enter key, substituting for the "OK" key located on the left side of the camera. However, unlike the OK button, the center button has the capability to be reprogrammed to serve an alternative function under particular circumstances.

4. The "OK" button: To ensure consistency, the enter function should be executed using the OK button instead of the multi selector center button. While it can be utilized in conjunction with other controls during playback (e.g., OK+Up to toggle card locations), its functionalities remain largely unaltered and cannot be reassigned.

5. The Sub-Selector Control: This control, while capable of being modified to navigate menu options, is primarily designed to be a convenient control for setting the focus point. Additionally, it can be squeezed inward to secure focus or exposure.

6. The Main Command and Sub Command dials: They are located in the front and rear of the Z8. The main control dial is employed to alter parameters such as the shutter speed, whereas the sub control dial is utilized to modify an alternative or secondary option. For instance, in Manual exposure mode, the aperture is adjusted via the sub-command dial, whereas the shutter speed is modified via the main command dial. (The dial is only "active" for these adjustments in both instances when the Z8's exposure meter is engaged.) The meter will enter a dormant state after a specified period of time; to

reactivate it and access the main and sub-command dials, you will need to press the shutter release button on the camera.

How to Use the Touchscreen

The tilting LCD display accommodates an extensive range of touch operations. During the initial setup process, the touchscreen will also be required. On the other hand, the touch screen could prove to be extraordinarily useful when playing back images or filming in live view. The following is a compilation of action you can carry out with the touch screen:

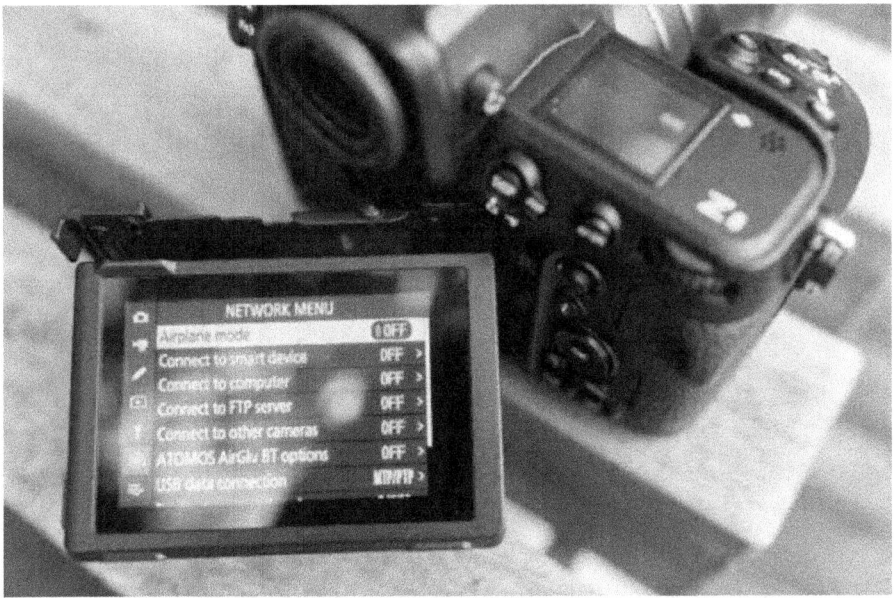

1. When in Playback Mode

-   Flip through images: You can navigate to different images during playback by swiping the screen.

- Zoom in and out: To adjust the magnification of an image for closer inspection, perform a double-tap on the touch screen.

- Relocate the magnified area: Swiping your finger across the display will relocate the zoomed area.

- Accessing thumbnails and movies: Additionally, users have the ability to navigate through thumbnails by scrolling on the screen.

2. In Live View Mode (LVM):

- Perform photography: An image can be taken in Live View mode by touching the display instead of holding down the shutter button.

- Select a focus point: You can select a focus point in both Live View and Movie modes by touching a location on the touch screen.

- Adjust white balance: By touching the display, you can designate a region for white balance computation.

3. In Shooting Mode:

- Navigate menus in Shooting Mode: In place of pressing the multidirectional button, use the touchscreen to navigate the menu options.

- Typing Text: Tap the on-screen keyboard to enter text when interacting with a text input panel (for instance, to enter copyright information in the Setup menu). This approach significantly expedites the process compared to tediously adjusting the focus between characters via the directional controls.

Nevertheless, touch features can be completely deactivated or restricted to playback functions only. Additionally, the Touch Controls option permits the configuration of full-frame playback "flicks" in either the left/right or right/left direction. Additionally, you can disable the Touch Shutter/AF function during live view and video recording by selecting an icon on the screen's left. If modifications are applicable, you will see a touch-sensitive white area displayed around the indication. In addition to the up/down and left/right triangles used to modify increments, there will be additional iconography presented for alternative functions.

4. Touchscreen Gestures that are available include:

-   Flick: Move a single finger laterally across the display. It should be noted that the display will remain motionless if another finger or other object contacts it. During playback, a motion to the right or left advances to the subsequent or preceding image, respectively.

-   Slide: To slide, move a single finger across the screen in a leftward, rightward, upward, or downward direction. You can use this motion to navigate within a magnified image while playing.

- Stretch/Squeeze: To enlarge an image while it is playing, spread two fingers apart, or press your fingertips together to enlarge it.

- Tap: To alter a menu which you have selected, touch the display with one finger. Utilize the up/down or left/right triangles to adjust settings like display brightness. If Touch Shutter is active in live view, tapping the screen sets the focus point and captures a photo upon lifting your finger. When Touch Shutter is off, screen touch only shifts the focus point.

Having familiarized yourself with using certain camera controls, proceed to fully configure your camera by following the steps below:

Setting the Language:

Many languages are supported by the Z8. Given that distributors may have partially configured the camera, it is highly probable that it is already localized to the language spoken in their area. To modify the language, proceed as follows:

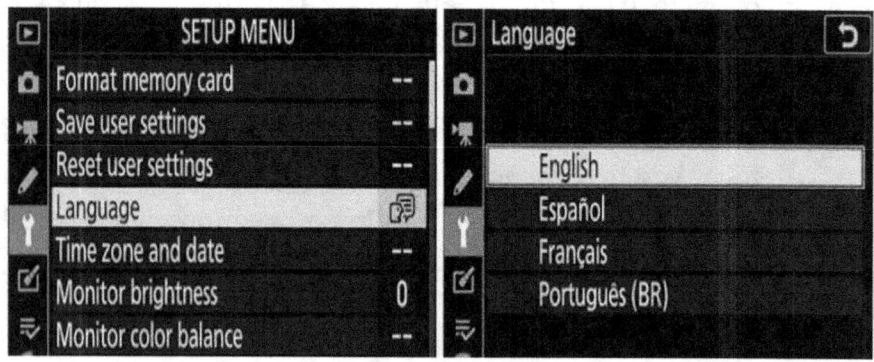

1. To begin, locate the Setup Menu and select it.

2. Click on the Language option, then proceed by scrolling to the right.

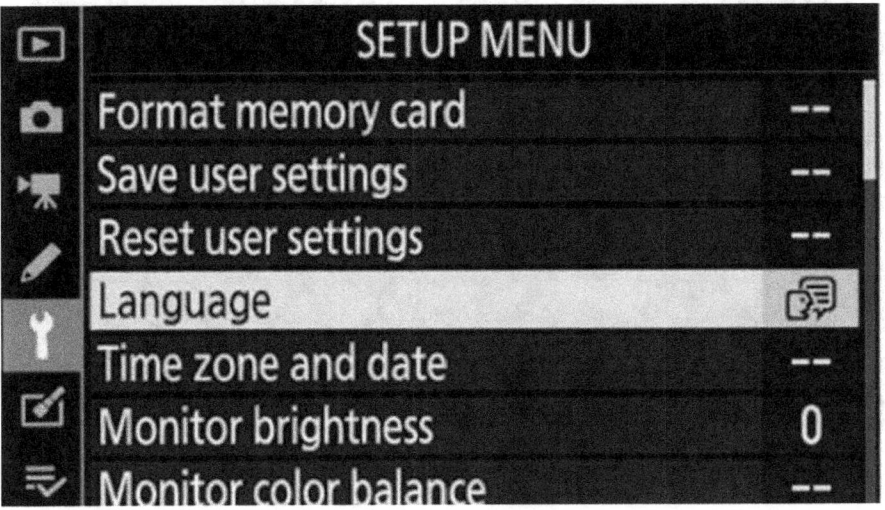

3. To navigate through the list where you will choose a specific language, manipulate the circular Multi selector pad located at the rear of the camera in an upward or downward direction. To select a language of your choice, press the OK button on the bottom left of the camera or the Multi selector center button, which is situated in the center of the Multi selector pad.

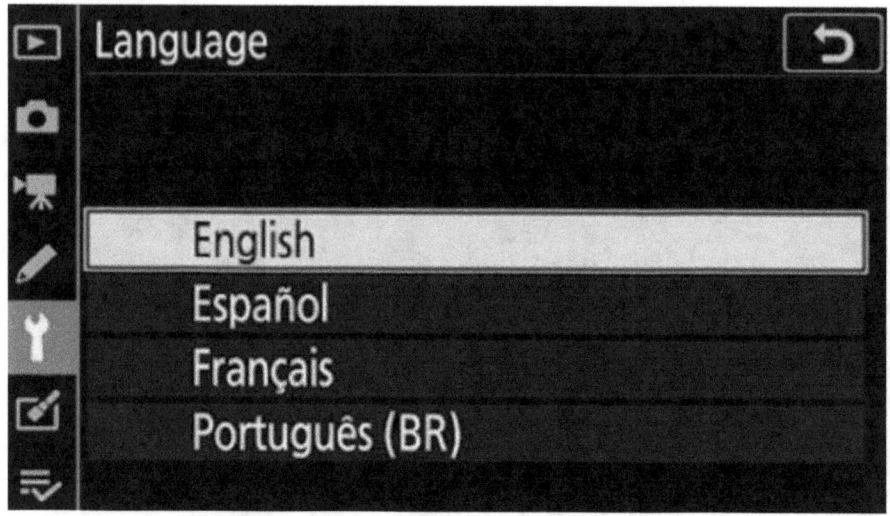

- **Choosing the Time Zone and Date**

To select the proper time zone for your location, follow the subsequent steps:

1. In the Setup Menu screen flow, select the third screen

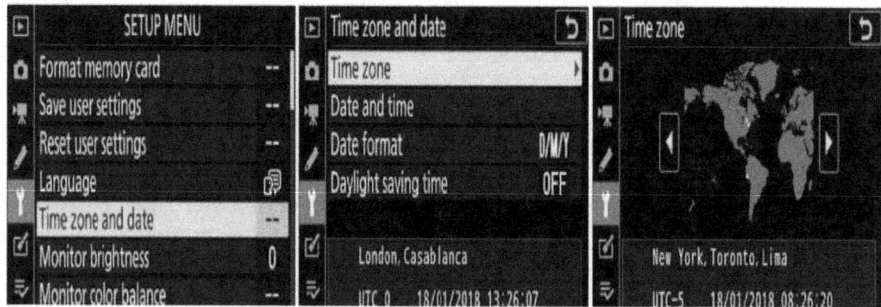

2. Slide the Multi Selector pad to the left or right until the current location is highlighted in yellow. Afterwards, you will

observe either a vertical yellow stripe or a faint yellow outline accompanied by a red dot. The currently specified time zone will be indicated in the bottom-right corner of the screen. After ensuring that your time zone is set, click the OK icon. After choosing your time zone, proceed to follow the next steps to set up your date and time according to that selected time zone.

3. In the Setup Menu screen flow, select the third screen

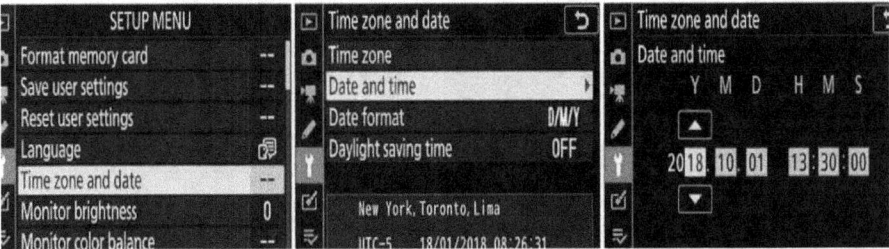

4. To browse between the various sections containing dates and times, scroll left or right using the Multi selector pad. To modify their respective parameters, navigate vertically or laterally. The time values are expressed on a 24-hour military timepiece. After entering the date and time, proceed by selecting the OK button. Next, follow the instructions below to set the format for the date and time;

5. In the Setup Menu screen flow, select the third screen

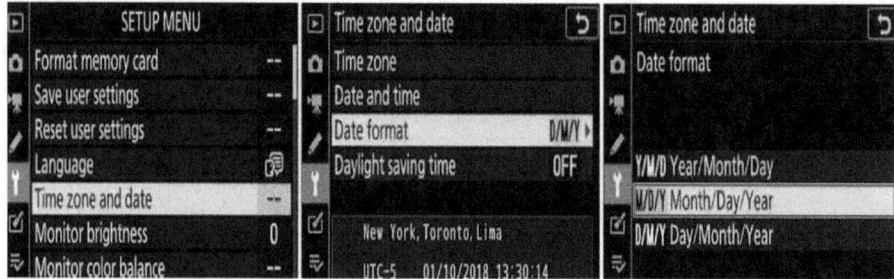

6. To select the desired date format, navigate up or down using the Multi selector pad. To choose the desired format, press the OK button.

Charging and Inserting a Battery into the Camera

Your Nikon Z8 is an intricate electronic device that functions exclusively with a charged battery.

A flashing indicator light will illuminate once the battery has been inserted into the MH-25a charger in the correct manner. This flickering will continue for about 2.5 hours or until the status indicator illuminates continuously, at which point the charging will be complete.

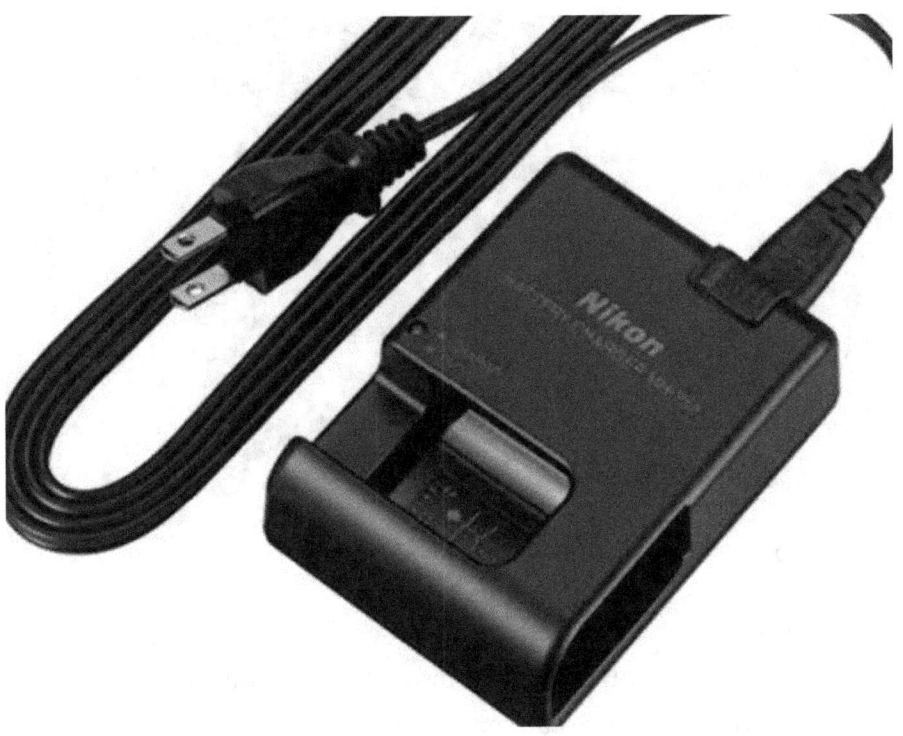

Once the battery has been charged, insert it into the camera by opening the lever on its bottom.

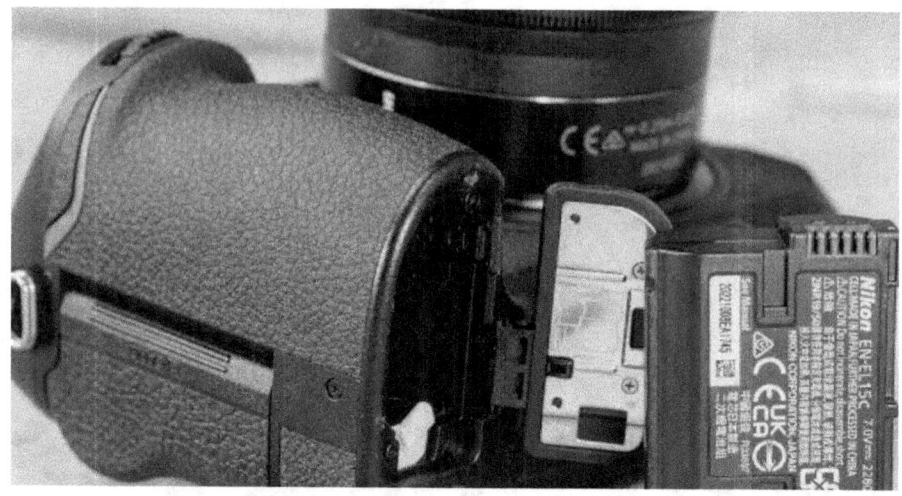

- **How to Mount the Lens**

After selecting your desired lens, loosen it, but keep the rear lens cover in place. If you vertically insert the lens into the designated compartment within the camera case, it not only ensures that it is accessible for immediate use but also safeguarded against unintended incidents. The posterior portion of the lens remains concealed until the rear lens cover is released, enabling a last-second release and subsequent removal from the lens's rear.

To detach the body cover, rotate it away from the release mechanism. Remove the rear lens cover from the lens as well as the body cap, then set it aside. Proceed with the lens installation process by ensuring that the raised white protrusion on the lens mount is in alignment with the alignment indication on the lens barrel. Rotate the lens until it is securely positioned in the direction of the shutter release button. Some lenses, particularly telephotos and telephoto zooms equipped with swiveling collars for tripod attachment, pose a greater challenge during installation. To avoid any collision between the tripod foot and the Z8's prism front overhang, you must adjust the collar.

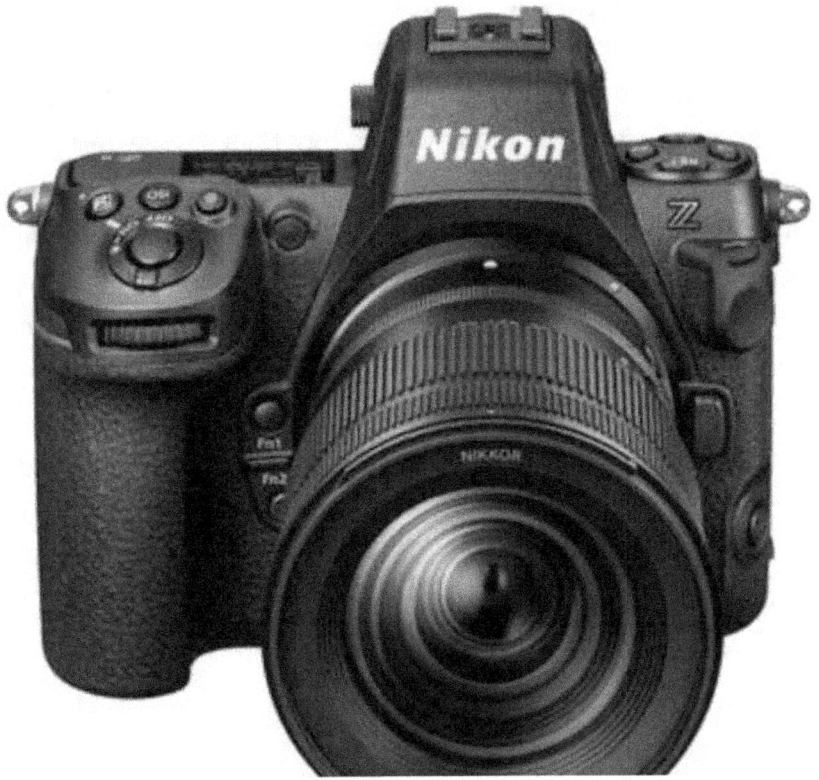

Change the focus mode switch to M-AF (autofocus) or AF (autofocus) once the lens has been attached. By bayoneting the lens in the opposite position, the lens hood can be unscrewed and reattached with the "petals" (present on nearly all lens hoods for contemporary Nikon optics) facing outward. This feature facilitates the travel-compactibility of the lens and hood combination. Lens coverings reduce flare caused by light from beyond the image region striking the lens and prevent unintended disturbances to the front portion of the lens.

How to Adjust the Diopter Control

Individuals with minimal visual impairment can benefit from a small measure of optical correction via the viewfinder. However, if you already wear contact lenses or spectacles, the diopter correction may not require modification. Nonetheless, if you prefer to use the Z8 without your spectacles, the camera features an integrated diopter adjustment that spans a range of -2 to +1. Once the eye is clearly focused on the subject through the viewfinder, rotate the diopter adjustment dial adjacent to it until the image is crystal clear. If you wish to effectively assess focus through the viewfinder, you should utilize an actual image rather than the status indicators, as the optical distance between the focus screen, where your subject appears, and the indicators located outside the image region is slightly different.

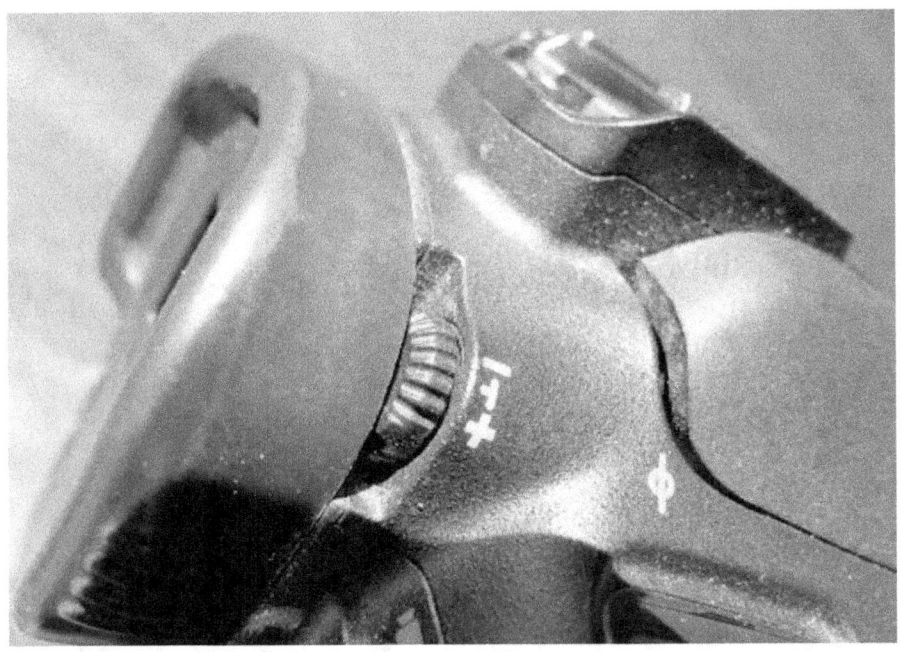

In the event that there are different users of one camera, and one user desires a distinct diopter positioning on a shared camera with others, it is advisable to track the number of touches and rotations (clockwise to increase the diopter effect; counterclockwise to decrease the diopter significance) necessary to transition between users. Also, should the Diopter correction be insufficient, Nikon offers nine alternative Diopter-Adjustment Viewfinder Correction lenses for the viewfinder window, with prices ranging from approximately $16 to +3.

How to Insert a Memory Card

To insert the memory card, disengage the memory card cover by sliding the door on the back-right border of the body toward the rear of the camera, and then open it. It is imperative to remove a memory card only when the camera is in the off position or the yellow-green memory access indicator, which signifies card writing, is not illuminated.

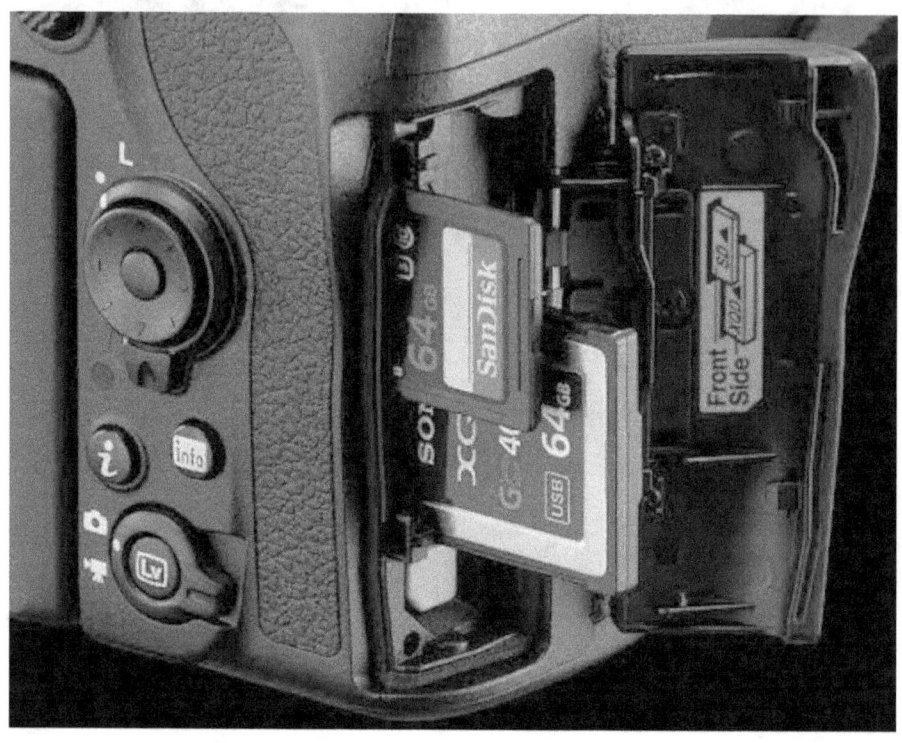

Inside the memory card area, there are two card slots: one for XQD cards at the bottom and one for SD media at the top. It is recommended to install the XQD card with the label facing the rear of the camera and in such a way that the edge bearing the contacts enters the opening initially. Conversely, you can remove a memory card by simply forcing it inward; thereafter, it will protrude towards you, allowing you to remove it.

How to Format a Memory Card

Formatting a memory card for a brand-new camera can be done in two ways:

1. Formatting via the Setup Menu: Right-click the multi selector and navigate to the Format Memory Card entry by pressing the MENU icon.

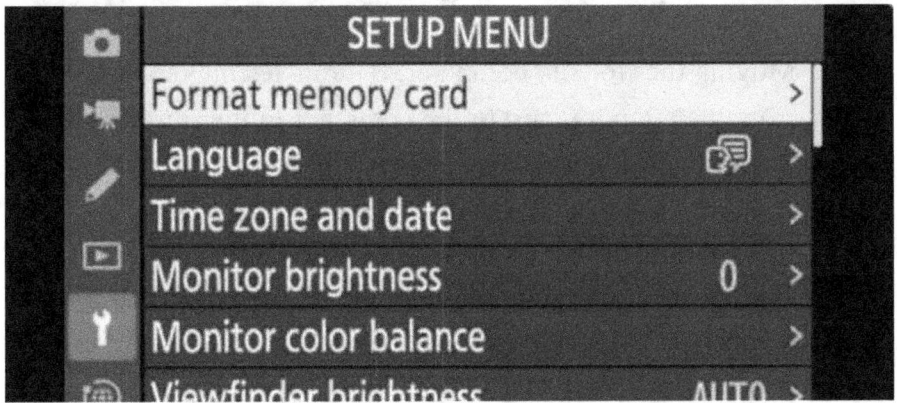

Select either the SD or XQD memory card, depending on the one you want to be formatted. Then click Yes in the resulting interface. Additionally, the wrench-icon which represents the Setup menu can be accessed via the thumb-pad-sized control located to the right of the LCD display. Press OK to initiate the formatting procedure.

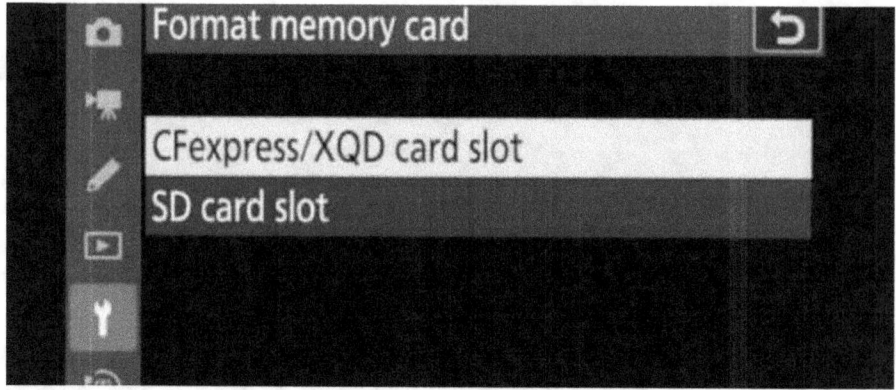

2. Moving files to your computer: By transferring the image files from the memory card to the computer (either through a card reader or a direct cable transfer), the card is devoid of any content and the previous image files are removed. Nevertheless, this approach fails to eliminate protected files and fails to detect and restrict access to regions of the memory card that have undergone corruption or rendered them inoperable subsequent to the most recent card formatting. Therefore, it is recommended that whenever you wish to create a blank card, you format the card rather than simply transferring the image files. However, you can use this method when you desire for the protected/unerased images to remain on the card for an extended period of time, for the purpose of sharing them with family, friends, and so forth.

CAMERA CONTROLS, BUTTONS, AND FEATURES

Controls, Buttons and Features on the Top Side

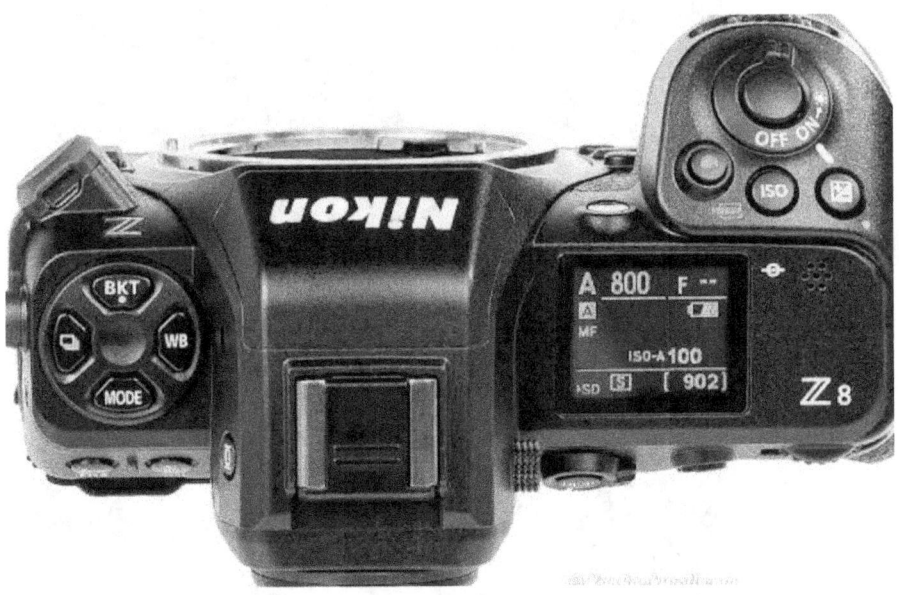

1. BKT Button: When bracketing, use this button in conjunction with the Main Command Dial and Sub-Command Dial to determine the number of frames and the transition.

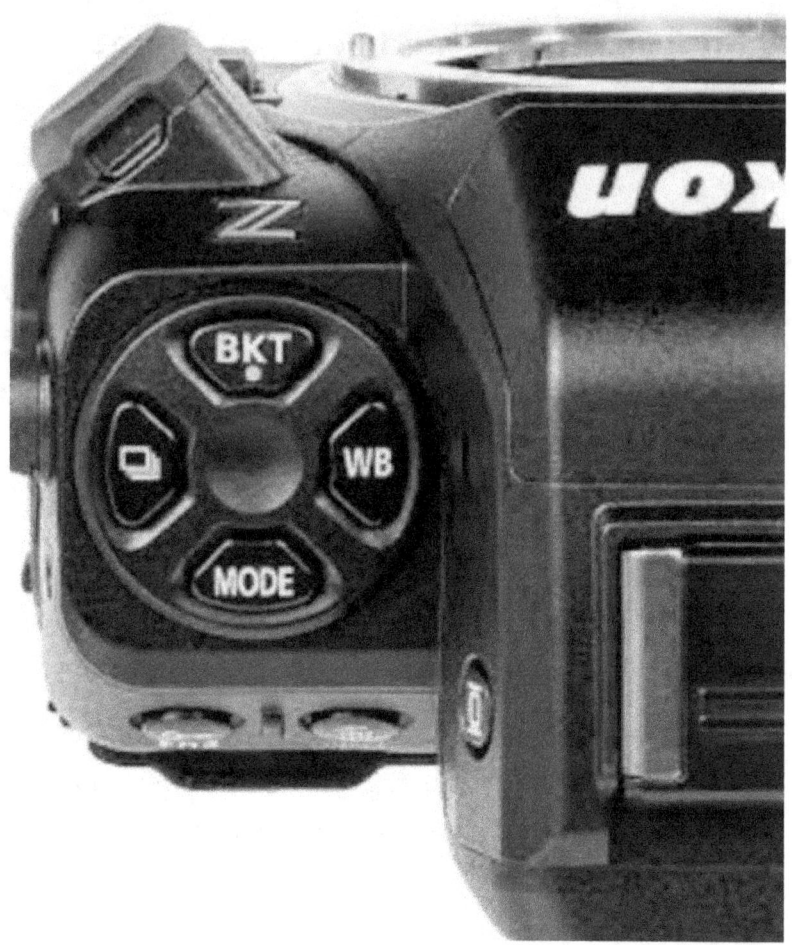

2. WB Button: To adjust the white balance, press this button followed by a rotation of the Main Command Dial or Sub-Command Dial.

3. Stereo Microphones: They are utilized during video making to capture audio.

4. The Video Record Button: This initiates and terminates video recording when the camera is set to video mode.

5. Shutter Release Button: To initiate autofocus, press this button halfway down; to capture a picture, press it all the way down.

6. The On/Off Switch: This is a toggle that controls the camera's power state.

7. ISO Button: To adjust the ISO setting, press this button while rotating the main command dial.

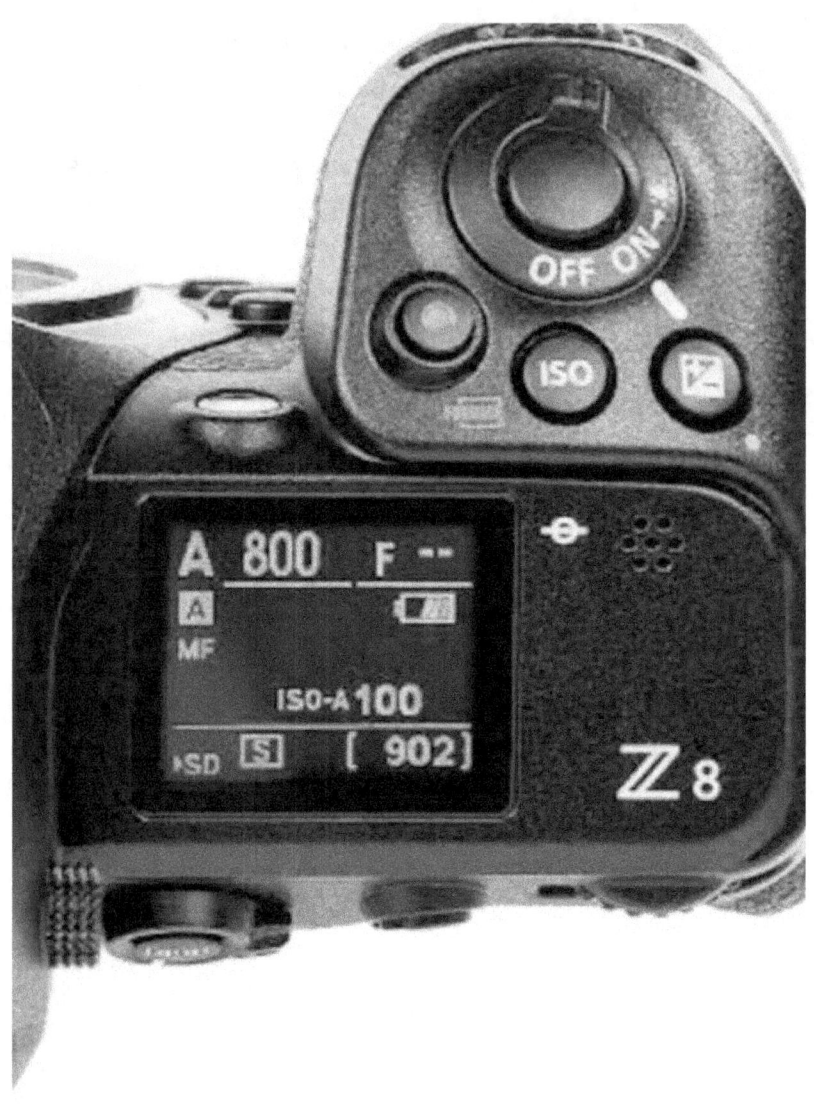

8. Exposure Compensation Button: To adjust the exposure compensation, press this button while simultaneously rotating the main command dial.

9. Speaker: This component is utilized to provide audio output from the camera.

10. Control Panel: This displays the camera's current settings.

11. Diopter Adjustment: This component is utilized to modify the diopter of the viewfinder.

12. The Monitor Mode Button: The function of the monitor mode button is to toggle between the viewfinder and monitor displays.

13. Mode Button: To toggle between P (Programmed Auto), A (Aperture Priority), S (Shutter Speed Priority), and M (Manual), press this button and rotate the Main Command Dial.

14. Release Mode Button: In conjunction with the Main Command Dial, press this button to alter the release mode setting of the Release Mode Dial.

Controls, Buttons and Features at the Back Side

The following is a list of the back controls and their respective functions:

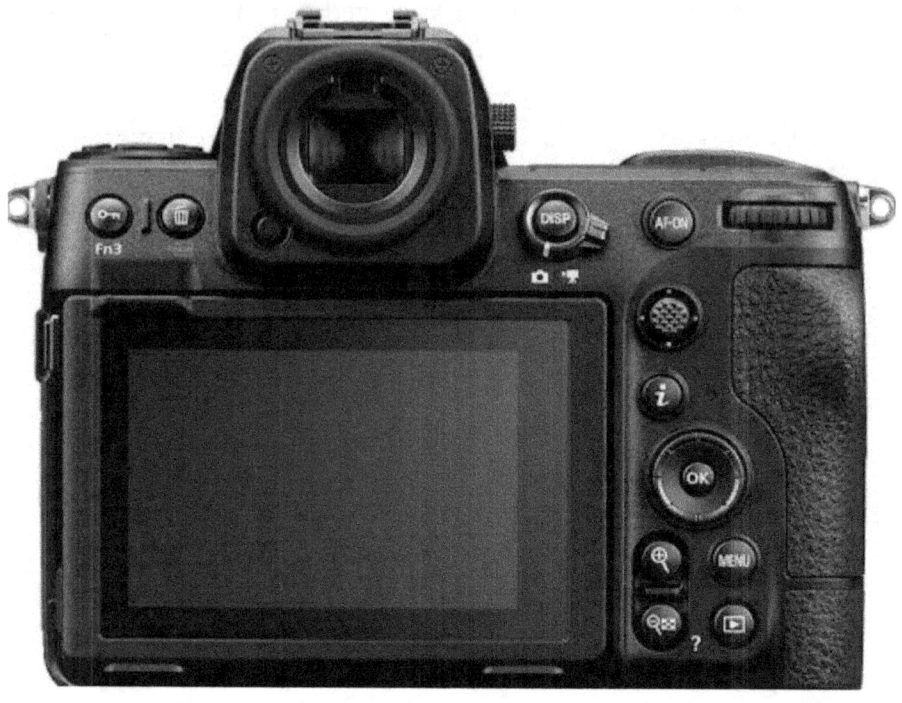

1. Eye Sensor: When the eye is in the viewfinder, the eye sensor toggles the display from the monitor to the viewfinder.

2. The DISP Button: This button is utilized to navigate between different display panels.

3. Photo/Video Selector Button: This button is utilized to toggle between the photo and video modes.

4. The Sub-selector: This functions as a joystick for determining the focus point. In order to secure focus and exposure, press and hold.

5. AF-ON Button: To enable autofocus, press this button.

6. The Main Command Dial: This dial is used to modify the camera's parameters.

7. The iButton: the function of the i-button is to access the camera Menus settings, but such settings depend on the camera mode.

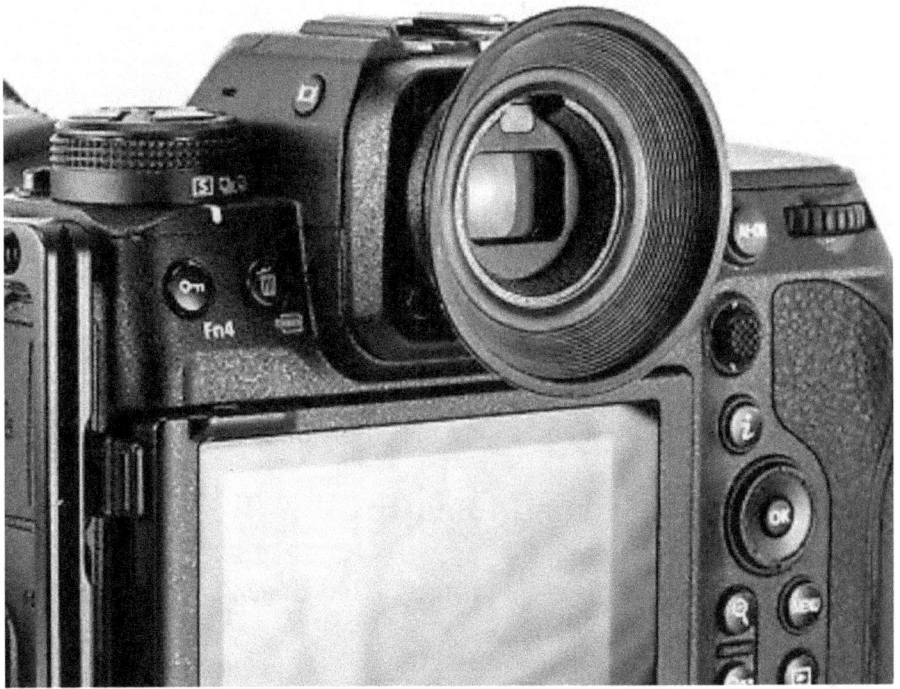

8. The "OK" button: This is utilized to confirm the option that you have selected.

9. Multi Selector: To navigate menus or select AF points, press this button.

10. Magnify Button: Utilize the magnify button to enlarge the image currently displayed on the LCD.

11. Menu Button: To access and deactivate the camera's menu system, press this button.

12. The Zoom Out button: This is utilized to enlarge the present image displayed on the LCD.

13. The Playback Button: This button displays the most recent image captured on the LCD.

14. Trash: This is utilized to delete the current image from the LCD.

15. Protect/Fn3 Button: To safeguard the current image during playback, press this button; to configure Picture Controls, press this button and rotate the Main Command Dial.

Controls, Buttons and Features at the Front Side

The buttons and controls at the front side have been explained below;

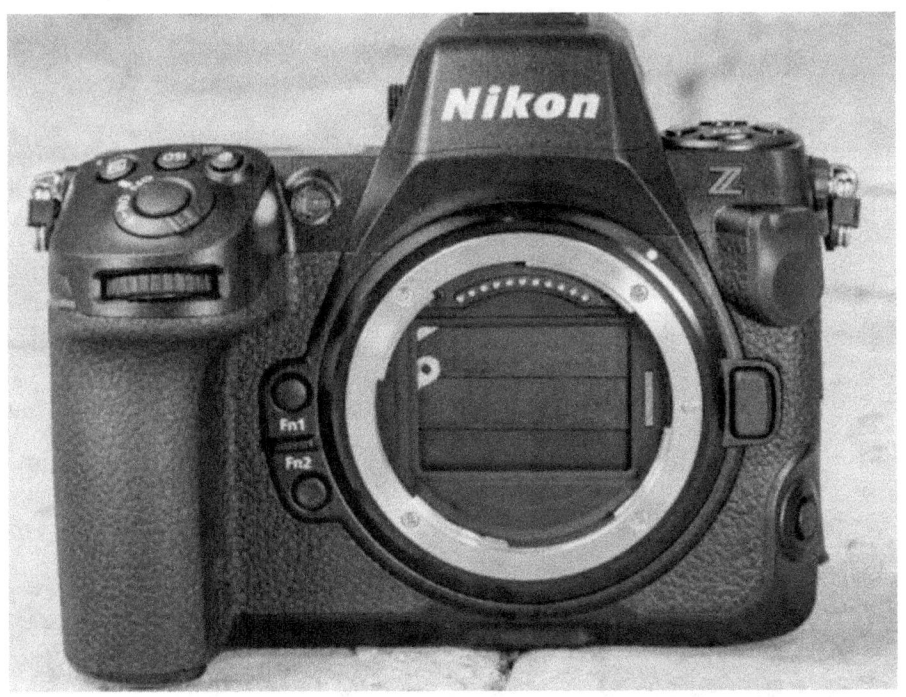

1. The Sub Command Dial: The purpose of the sub-command dial is to modify several options in the camera.

2. 10-Pin Remote Terminal (under cover): This is where a 10-pin remote is connected.

3. External Microphone Connector (located beneath the side cover): This port is used to connect external microphones.

4. Headphone Connector: This port is concealed on the side and is used to connect external headphones.

5. HDMI Connector (located beneath the side cover): This is used to connect an HDMI cable.

6. USB Data Connector: Under the side cover is a USB data connector through which a data cable can be connected.

7. USB Power Connector (located beneath the side cover): This port accepts a USB power supply cable.

8. Focus Mode Button: In order to alter the focus mode, press this button and rotate the Main Command Dial.

9. The Battery Chamber Cover: This is the location where the battery is inserted.

10. Fn2 Button: By default, the Fn2 button can be programmed to select the "Choose Image Area" option.

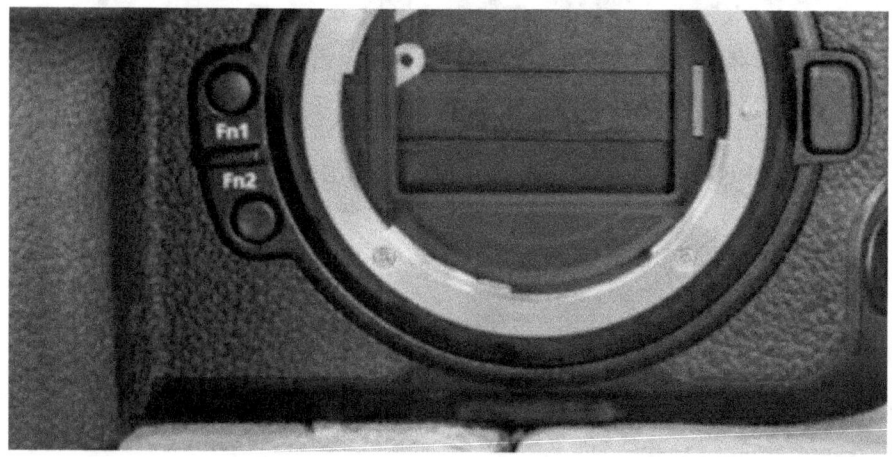

11. Fn1 Button: The "Shooting Menu Bank" default setting can be assigned to the Fn1 programmable button.

12. Memory card Slots: They are located beneath the side cover. These slots are utilized to insert the memory cards.

The Viewfinder Display (Photo)

The following information will be displayed on the viewfinder when you are shooting an image:

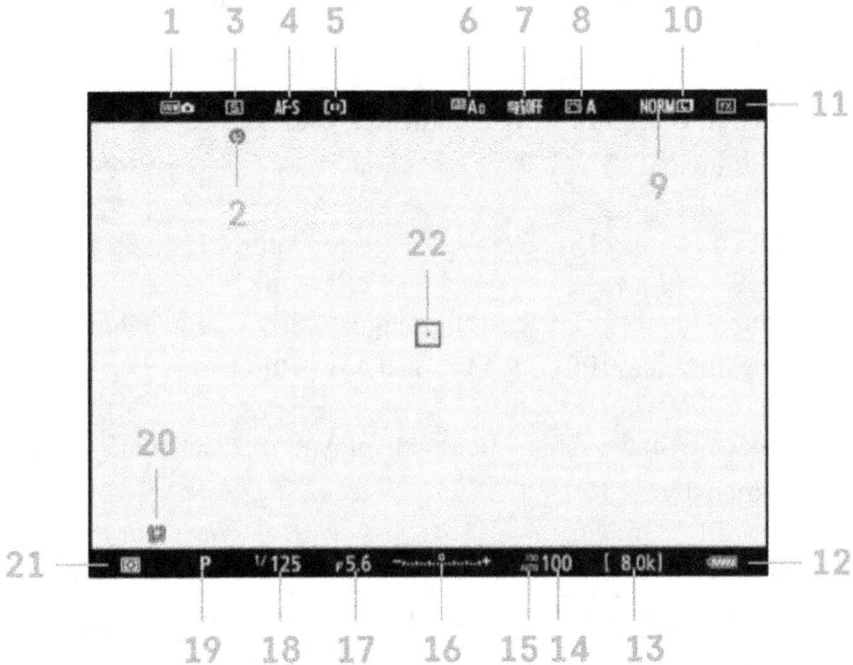

1. The View Mode: The Viewfinder displays the current view mode.

2. Clock Not Set Indicator: The flickering of the Clock Not Set Indicator signifies that the date and time have not been configured.

3. The Release Mode: This information indicates the present release mode.

4. Focus Mode: This variable indicates the present focus mode.

5. AF-Area Mode: The AF-area mode will also be displayed on the Viewfinder.

6. White Balance: This value indicates the present WB configuration.

7. Active D-Lighting: This indicates whether or not the scene is illuminated.

8. Picture Control: The current Picture Control is displayed.

9. Image Quality: The current image quality is indicated in thins. For instance, JPEG, RAW, or RAW+JPEG.

10. Image Size: This field displays the current image's dimensions.

11. Image Area: This parameter displays the current image area. For instance, FX denotes a full frame sensor and DX a cropped sensor.

12. Battery Indicator: This device exhibits the remaining battery capacity.

13. Number of Remaining Exposures: This indicates the quantity of photographs that can be captured with the current configuration and the memory card's available space.

14. ISO Sensitivity: This displays the most recent ISO.

15. The ISO/Auto ISO Sensitivity Indicator: This indicates whether or not Auto ISO is activated.

16. Indicator of Exposure and Exposure Compensation: This displays the current exposure and whether or not exposure compensation is in effect.

17. Aperture: This value represents the current aperture.

18. Shutter Speed: This value indicates the present shutter speed.

19. Shooting Mode: This displays the current shooting mode, for example, it may display either P, A, S, or M.

20. Indicator for Vibration Reduction: This signifies whether vibration reduction is activated.

21. Metering mode: The current metering mechanism is displayed.

22. Focus Point: This displays the chosen focus value.

Viewfinder Display (Movie)

The following data and visual representations will be presented on the viewfinder during filming:

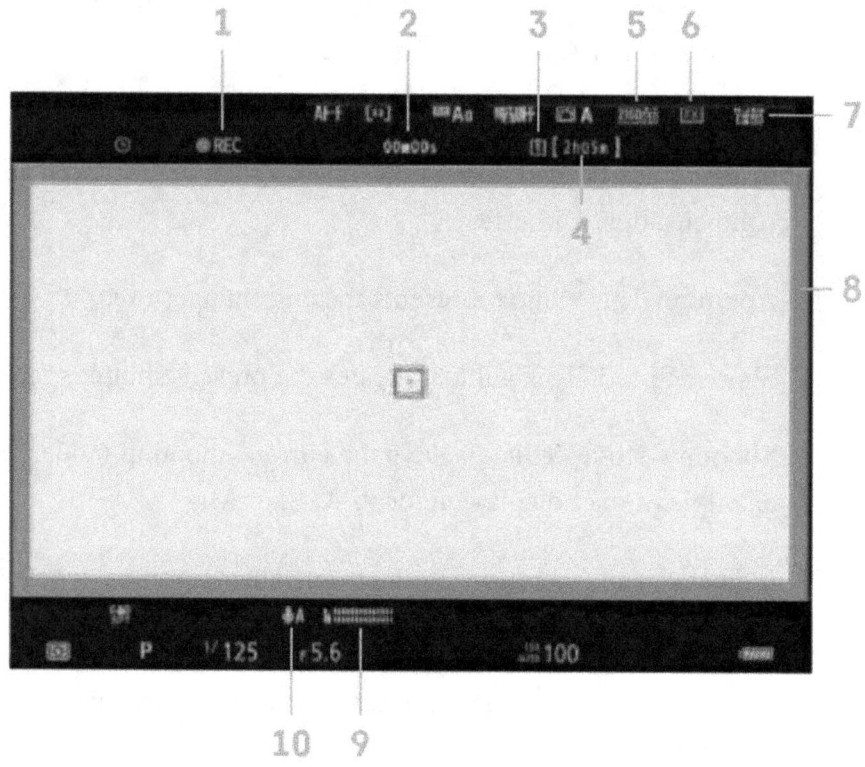

1. Recording Indicator / Recording Disabled: This function indicates whether or not a movie is being recorded. It also indicates when recording movies is not possible.

2. Video Recording Time: This indicates how long the video that is currently being recorded has been in progress.

3. Destination: This indicates the card location on which the video is being downloaded.

4. Time Remaining: This indicates, based on the existing parameters, the quantity of time until the memory card is complete.

5. Frame Rate and dimensions: This indicates the current frame rate and dimensions.

6. Image Area: This parameter displays the current image area. For instance, the DX or FX.

7. Video File Type: Indicates the form of video currently in use.

8. The Recording Indicator: This indicator illuminates when the camera is in the process of recording video and resembles a crimson border around the viewfinder.

9. Sound Level: This variable displays the present sound levels.

10. Sensitivity of the Microphone: This displays the current sensitivity settings for the microphone.

Monitor Display (Photo)

The following information and displays will appear on the monitor screen while a photograph is being taken:

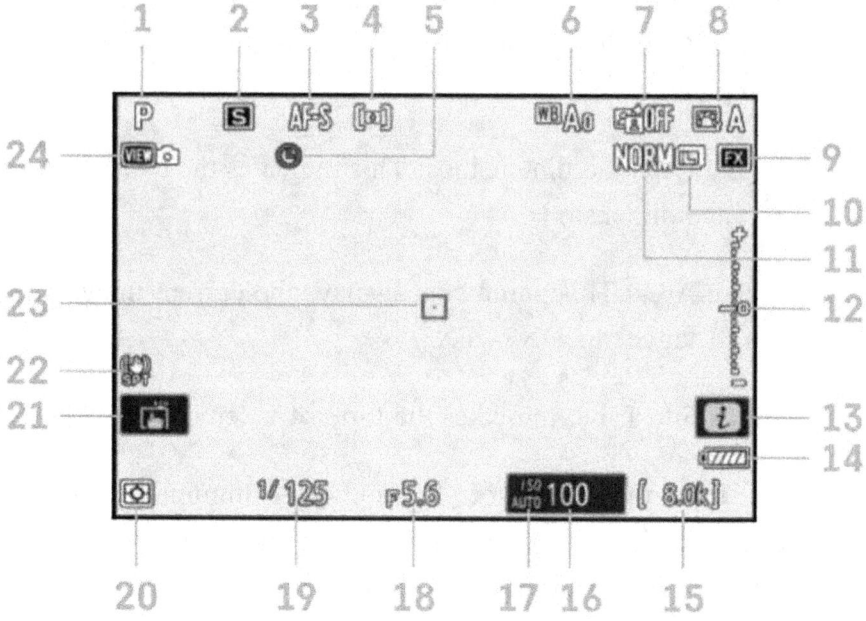

1. Shooting Mode: This variable indicates the current shooting option.

2. Release Mode: This parameter indicates the present release mechanism.

3. Focus Mode: This variable indicates the present mode which the camera is using to focus.

4. AF-Area Mode: This displays the current AF- Area value

5. Clock Not Set Indicator: A blinking clock not set indicator indicates that the date and time require setting.

42

6. White Balance: This value indicates the present WB configuration.

7. Active D-Lighting: This indicates whether or not D-Lighting is active.

8. Picture Control: The current Picture Control is displayed here.

9. Image Area: This parameter displays the current image area. For instance, FX represents a full frame sensor and DX a cropped sensor.

10. Image Size: The current image size is displayed here.

11. Image Quality: This indicates the current image format and quality, including JPEG, RAW+JPEG, or RAW.

12. Indicator of Exposure and Exposure Compensation: This displays the current exposure and whether or not exposure compensation is in effect.

13. i symbol: Tapping the i symbol will launch the i Menu.

14. Battery Indicator: This device exhibits the remaining battery capacity.

15. Number of Remaining Exposures: This indicates the quantity of photographs that can be captured with the current configuration and the memory card's available space.

16. Auto ISO Sensitivity Indicator: Indicates whether Auto ISO is enabled.

17. ISO Sensitivity: Displays the current ISO ISO status.

18. Aperture: This value represents the current aperture

19. Shutter Speed: This value indicates the present shutter speed

20. Metering Mode: The current metering mechanism is displayed.

21. Touch Shooting: This indicates whether or not Touch Shooting is activated.

22. The Vibration Reduction indicator: This indicates whether or not VR is activated.

23. Focus Point: This indicates which focus point is selected.

24. View Mode: This attribute displays the current view mode.

Monitor Display (Movie)

The monitor display will exhibit the following information and displays while a movie is being shot:

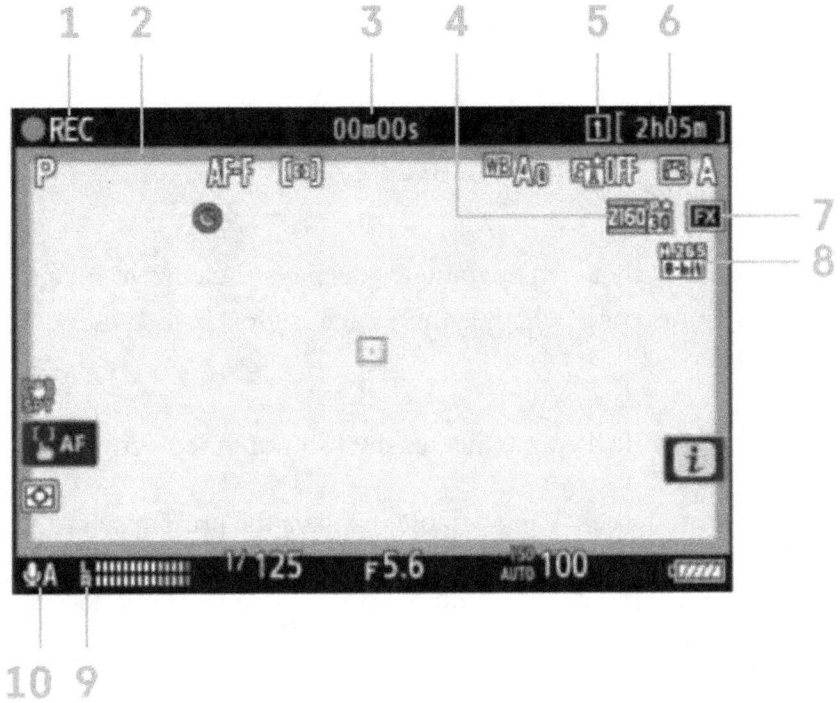

1. The "Recording Indicator" or "Recording Disabled" status: This indicates whether or not a movie is being recorded.

2. Recording Indicator: A crimson border appears around the display to indicate that the camera is currently recording video.

3. Video Recording Time: This indicates how long the video that is currently being recorded has been in progress.

4. Frame Rate and dimensions: This indicates the current frame rate and dimensions.

45

5. Destination: This indicates the card location on which the video is being downloaded.

6. Time Remaining: This indicates, based on the existing parameters, the quantity of time until the memory card is complete.

7. Image Area: This parameter displays the current image area. For instance, whether the image region is located on FX or DX.

8. Video File Type: Indicates the form of video currently in use.

9. Sound Level: This variable displays the present sound levels.

10. Sensitivity of the Microphone: This displays the current sensitivity settings for the microphone.

Control Panel

The following information and displays will be presented on the control interface during shooting:

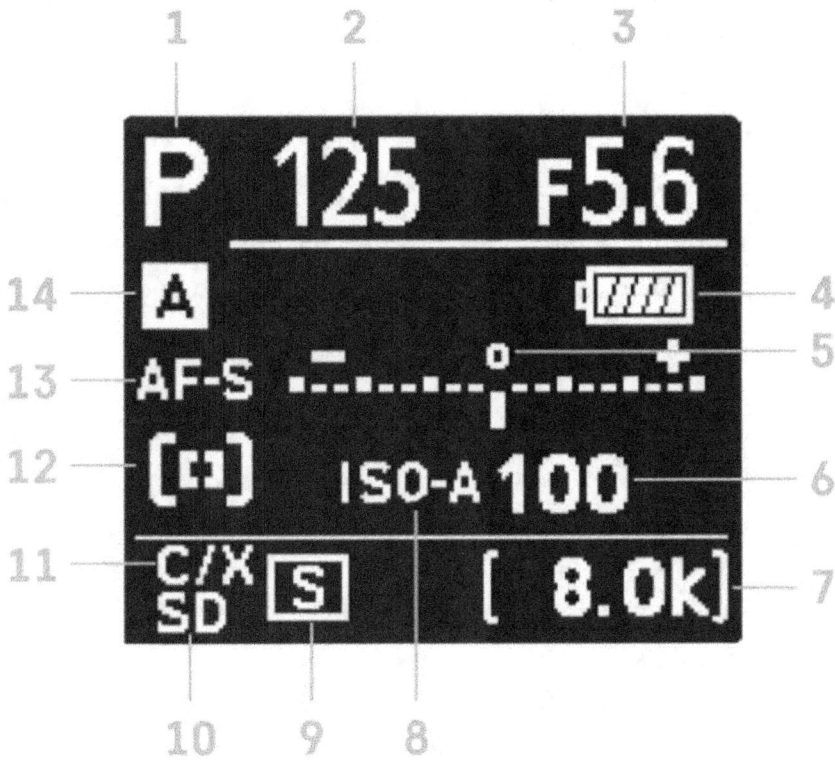

1. Shooting Mode: This variable indicates the shooting mode that is currently in use.

2. Shutter Speed: This value indicates the present shutter rate.

3. Aperture: This value represents the present rate of aperture.

4. Battery Indicator: This is where the present battery level is exhibited.

5. Exposure Indicator: This displays the impact of the current exposure settings.

6. ISO: This displays the present ISO standard.

7. The "Number of Exposures Remaining" or "Available Recording Time": This indicates the quantity of video footage that can be captured at the present time and under the current conditions.

8. The ISO Sensitivity Indicator: This indicates whether or not Auto ISO is activated.

9. Release Mode: This value indicates the present release mode.

10. SD Card Memory Slot (2): Indicates the currently specified card slots.

11. CFexpress / XQD Memory Slot (1): Indicates the currently selected card slots.

12. The Af-Area Mode Indicator: This displays the AF-area mode which is presently in use.

13. Focus Mode: This variable indicates the present focus value.

14. Shooting Menu Bank: Indicates the currently selected menu bank.

ABOUT THE THE Z8 EXPOSURE MODE

Exposure is, at its most fundamental level, about light. Adequate exposure enhances the visibility of specific details within the subject area, thereby furnishing the necessary spectrum of hues and tones to reconstruct the intended photograph. Inadequate exposure can obscure critical details or obscure them with glare-filled, featureless expanses of white. However, achieving the ideal exposure requires some intelligence, due to the fact that digital sensors are incapable of capturing every conceivable tone. When an image contains a wide spectrum of tones, including intense black shadows and brilliant highlights, it is often necessary to choose an exposure that renders the majority of those tones, but not all, in a manner that is optimal for the intended photograph.

You likely possess knowledge regarding the conventional "exposure triangle" for Z-series mirrorless cameras. This triangle consists of three components: aperture (the quantity of light passing through the lens), shutter speed (the duration of time the shutter is open), and the ISO sensitivity of the sensor. These elements function in a proportional and reciprocal manner to generate an exposure. The trio's performance is influenced by the quantity of available illumination. Thus, you will obtain twice as much exposure if you double the quantity of light, increase the aperture by one stop, prolong the shutter speed by two stops, or increase the ISO setting by two stops. Likewise, to maintain the same level of exposure, one can increase one of these factors while decreasing the other by an equivalent magnitude.

When utilizing any of the three controls, compromises are inevitable. By means of the diffraction effect, larger f/stops result in reduced depth-of-field, whereas smaller f/stops increase depth-of-field and diminish sharpness. A greater reduction in the effects of camera/subject motion is achieved with shorter shutter speeds, whereas motion blur is more probable with lengthier shutter speeds. An image captured at a higher ISO will contain more visual noise and anomalies, whereas one captured at a lower ISO will have fewer noise-related issues.

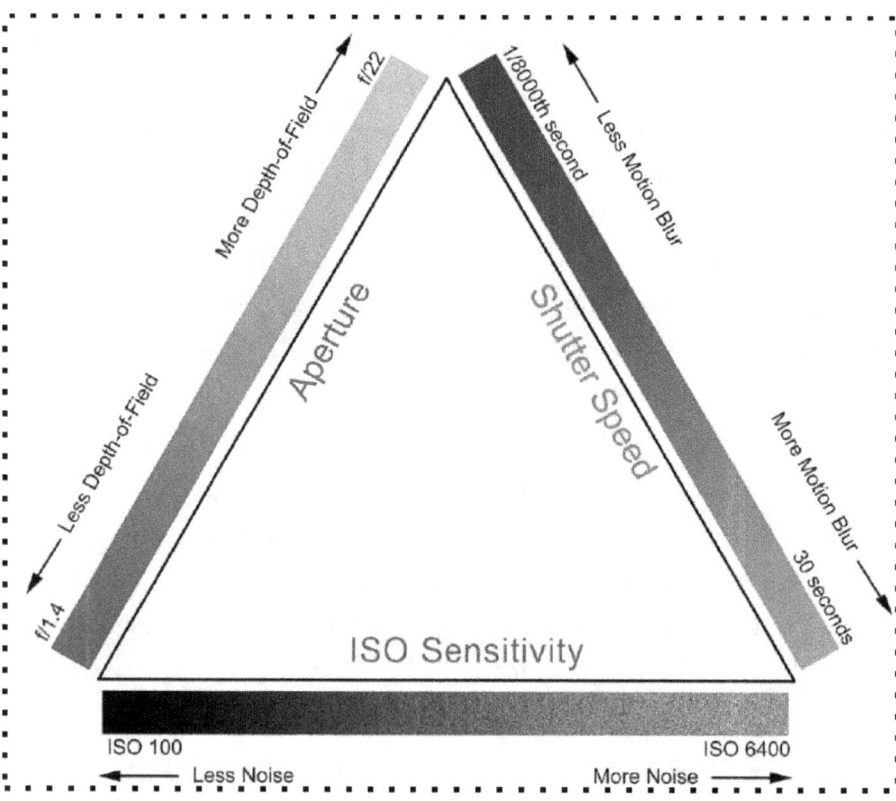

A comprehensive comprehension of exposure necessitates an understanding of the six facets of light that interact in order to generate an image. Commence by identifying a light source, such as the sun, an interior lantern, an electronic flare, or the radiance emanating from a campfire. Subsequently, trace the light's trajectory as it traverses the camera, passes through the lens, and ultimately reaches the sensor that captures the illumination. The factors which are under our control, that influence exposure are as follows:

1. Light at its source: Both human vision and cameras, whether digital or analog, exhibit heightened sensitivity to the visible light portion of the electromagnetic spectrum. A number of significant attributes of light are pertinent to photography, including color and severity (which is predominantly determined by the light source's apparent scale when it illuminates a subject). However, with regard to exposure, the most crucial characteristic of a light source is its intensity. We may possess direct authority over intensity, as in the case of an electronic strobe output that can be adjusted manually or automatically, or an interior light that can be diminished or intensified. In certain circumstances, the ability to modify intensity may be restricted to indirect means, as is the case with sunlight, which can be rendered fainter through the introduction of reflective or translucent materials along its trajectory.

2. Light's duration: Most light sources are commonly perceived as continuous. For instance, when the primary light source in a photograph is an intermittent flash or other electronic flash,

the duration of light can change rapidly enough to affect the exposure.

3. Emitted, transmitted, or reflected light: Subjects can be composed and captured in photographs through the light that is reflected from the subjects towards the camera lens, transmitted (e.g., from translucent objects illuminated from behind), emitted (e.g., from a television screen or candle), or continuously or briefly emitted by the light source. When the amount of light that reaches the lens from the subject varies, the exposure must be adjusted. We can influence this portion of the equation by increasing the quantity of light that strikes or passes through the subject (e.g., by incorporating reflectors or supplementing light sources) or by amplifying the light that is emitted (e.g., by enhancing the luminosity of the luminous object).

4. The light passed by the lens: A portion of the light that enters the lens does not fully traverse its surface. Light can be partially blocked by filters prior to its entry into the lens. A variable-sized aperture is generated within the lens barrel by means of a diaphragm, which dilates and contracts to regulate the quantity of light entering the lens. Variation of the aperture size grants exposure control, whether to the user or to the auto exposure function of the camera. Note; f/stop refers to the aperture's relative magnitude.

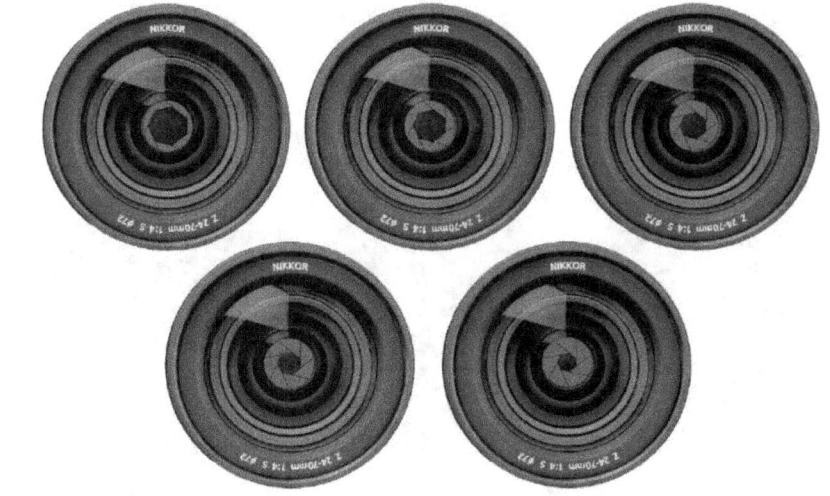

5. Light passing through the shutter: The duration of light transmission to the sensor is governed by the shutter speed, which can remain open for a short duration of 1/8000th of a second or for an extended period of 30 seconds—or even longer if the Bulb, Time, or extended shutter speeds settings are employed. These settings are located beyond the 30-second speed and are accessible exclusively in Manual exposure mode.

6. Light captured by the sensor: A portion of the light that strikes the sensor is not captured. Without data being recorded, a specific photosite will fail to receive a minimum number of photons that exceed a predetermined threshold. Likewise, in the event that an excessive amount of light strikes a pixel within the sensor, the surplus light either escapes detection or, more detrimentally, infiltrates neighboring pixels. By altering the ISO setting, it is possible to modify the minimum and

maximum pixel counts that contribute to the detail of an image. By amplification of incoming light at higher ISOs, the sensor's effective sensitivity will be enhanced.

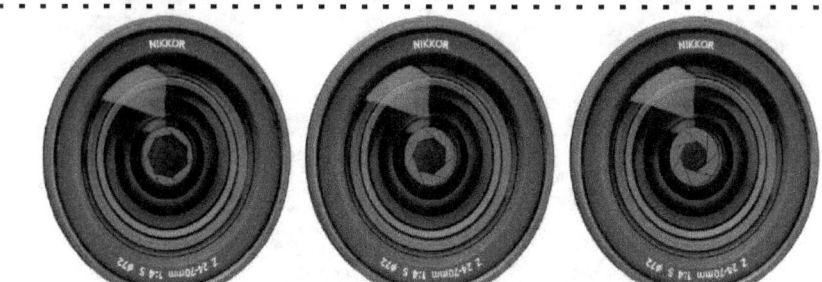

It is important to note that four of these factors; light quantity, light passing through the lens, shutter speed, and sensor sensitivity, all function in a proportional and reciprocal manner in order to generate an exposure. Additionally, you will obtain twice as much exposure if you increase the aperture size by one stop, the shutter speed by two stops, or the ISO sensitivity by two stops. In a similar fashion, any of these can be decreased to decrease the exposure when that is more desirable. Additionally, keep in mind that modifying any of these elements in P, A, or S mode does not affect the exposure, as the camera makes adjustments in order to maintain the same setting. Hence, as a result, Nikon offers alternative approaches to adjust the exposure in such modes.

F/stops And Shutter Speeds

For those who are relatively inexperienced with more sophisticated cameras, it will be useful to understand that the lens aperture, or f/stop, functions as a ratio akin to a fraction. This explains why f/2 is greater than f/4, just as 1/2 is greater than 1/4. In reality, f/2 is four times the magnitude of f/4. Typically, lenses are designated with intermediate f/stops denoting a size that is one-half or twice as large as the preceding aperture. For instance, the aperture of a lens could be denoted as follows: f/4, f/5.6, f/8, f/11, f/16; where each successive number signifies an aperture that permits half the amount of light as the previous one. Additionally, intermediate apertures, such as f/6.3 and f/7.1, which are situated between f/5.6 and f/8, can be configured.

The numerator is omitted from shutter velocities, which are expressed as actual fractions of a second. For example, the values 60, 125, 250, 500, 1,000, and so forth, denote 1/60th, 1/125th, 1/200th, 1/500th, and 1/1000th second, respectively. In order to prevent any potential confusion, Nikon designates longer exposures with quotation marks: 2, 2, 4.5, 4, and so forth, denoting exposures of 2.0, 2.5, and 4.0 seconds, respectively.

Equivalent Exposure

Typically, aperture and shutter speed are utilized to determine exposure, with ISO sensitivity being adjusted if the desired exposure cannot be obtained (i.e., the one that utilizes the "best" f/stop or shutter speed to achieve the desired depth-of-field or action halting).

An essential element to consider in this discourse is the concept of equivalent exposure. This concept denotes that the quantity of light that reaches the sensor remains constant across different aperture and shutter speed configurations. The quantity of light that reaches the sensor can remain constant regardless of whether a small aperture (large f/number) is paired with a long shutter speed or a broad aperture (small f/number) is utilized in conjunction with a rapid shutter speed.

The subsequent image serves as an illustration of equivalent exposure settings applied to a variety of shutter speeds and f/stops; that is to say, each of the enumerated combination of settings will yield an exposure that is precisely identical.

SHUTTER SPEED	F/STOP
1/30th second	f/22
1/60th second	f/16
1/125th second	f/11
1/200th second	f/8
1/500th second	f/5.6

SHUTTER SPEED	F/STOP
1/1000th second	f/4
1/2000th second	f/2.8
1/4000th second	f/2
1/8000th second	f/1.4

The metering system automatically determines the appropriate exposure when the camera is in P mode. However, an alternative exposure can be quickly obtained by rotating the main command dial until the desired equivalent exposure combination is visible. When using the "Flexible Program" function, an asterisk will appear next to the letter P. Recalling that to increase depth-of-field or decrease shutter speed, one must rotate the command dial to the left; conversely, to increase depth-of-field or decrease shutter speed, one must rotate the dial to the right. This will facilitate adjustments to the Flexible Program. Employing the Flexible Program is primarily necessary when adjusting the depth of field (DOF) and shutter speed. Note; this program shift mode is deactivated when Flash is utilized.

How to Correctly Calculate and Determine Exposure

Note, since the camera may lack a definitive method of determining its focus value. Therefore, it is required to calculate the appropriate exposure using some principles and certain assumptions. For instance, on metrics for calculating the exposure is that the average luminance of an entire scene, or a portion thereof, should decrease to a middle-gray hue. According to conventional usage, this tone contains approximately 18 percent gray. Unfortunately, although the human eye perceives the traditional 18 percent value as a shade of gray, the camera's calibration is for a slightly darker tone.

The exposure is determined by selecting specific areas of a predetermined pattern for measuring exposure. The calculation of exposure is predicated on the assumption that the reflectance of each area under consideration is approximately equivalent to that of a neutral gray card, which reflects a "middle" gray ranging from 12 to 18 percent. (A camera retailer's "gray cards" for photography contain an 18 percent gray tone. Your camera has been calibrated to detect a 12 percent gray area that is marginally darker. This "average" supposition of 12 to 18 percent gray is required due to the fact that various objects reflect varying quantities of light. When a photograph is taken of two cats, one of which is dark gray and the other white, the white cat may reflect five times more light than the gray cat. An exposure that focuses exclusively on the gray cat will result in the white cat appearing faded out, whereas an exposure that also includes the white cat will cause the gray cat to appear black. This is easier to comprehend when examining photographs of black subjects (those that reflect little light), subjects with a preponderance of intermediate tones, and subjects with high reflection.

1. Accurately exposed

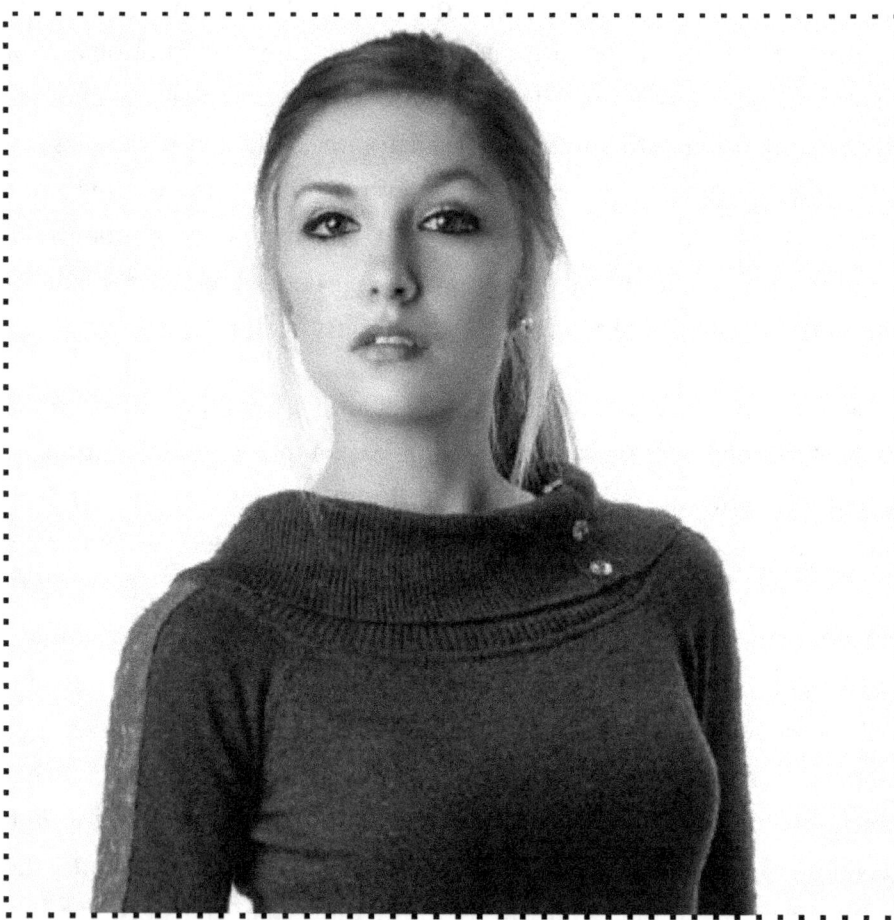

The image displayed above is an instance of an appropriately exposed image. The image depicts the potential appearance of a photograph in which the patches indicated at the bottom were inserted. Exposure was determined by measuring the light reflected from the middle-gray patch, which, for the purpose of illustration, is assumed to reflect around 12 to 18 percent of the incident light. The exposure meter within the camera detects an object that it interprets as a middle gray tone. Subsequently, it computes an exposure that accurately represents the tonal value of the patch situated in the center of the strip. Furthermore, the accurate rendering of the black patch on the left and the white patch on the right is a consequence of the appropriate exposure.

If, while taking photographs, the exposure meter calculates the light from an average of that "ideal" middle gray, then the obtained results will be comparable in accuracy. With the exception of subjects that are backlit or have irregular illumination, the exposure algorithms of the camera are modified to optimize the likelihood of achieving this type of result. Each of the three metering modes on the camera is optimized for a distinct category of peculiar subjects.

2. Overexposed

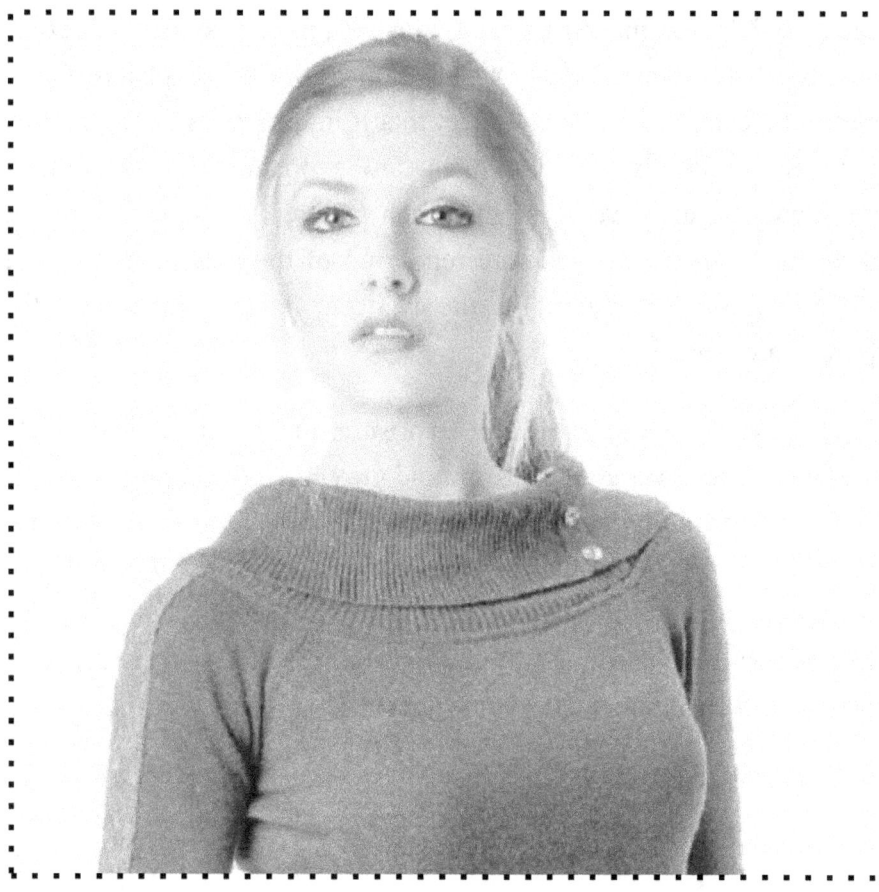

The image displayed above is a good example of an overexposed photograph. The image is a typical illustration of what would occur if the exposure were determined by metering the black region on the left. As the light meter detects comparatively less light reflected from the black square in contrast to a gray middle-tone subject, it will be necessary to increase exposure in order to bring the subject closer to a middle gray hue; resultantly, the "black" region becomes gray in color.

3. Poorly exposed

A third possibility is that the light meter could attempt to render the illumination reflected off the white region as a medium gray. Due to the white square's substantial light reflection, the exposure is diminished, bringing the affected area closer to a medium gray hue. The previously gray and black regions have been rendered excessively dark. Measuring the gray card, or an equivalent substitute that reflects approximately the same amount of light, is unquestionably the sole method to guarantee accurate exposure. The picture shown below is an instance of underexposed image.

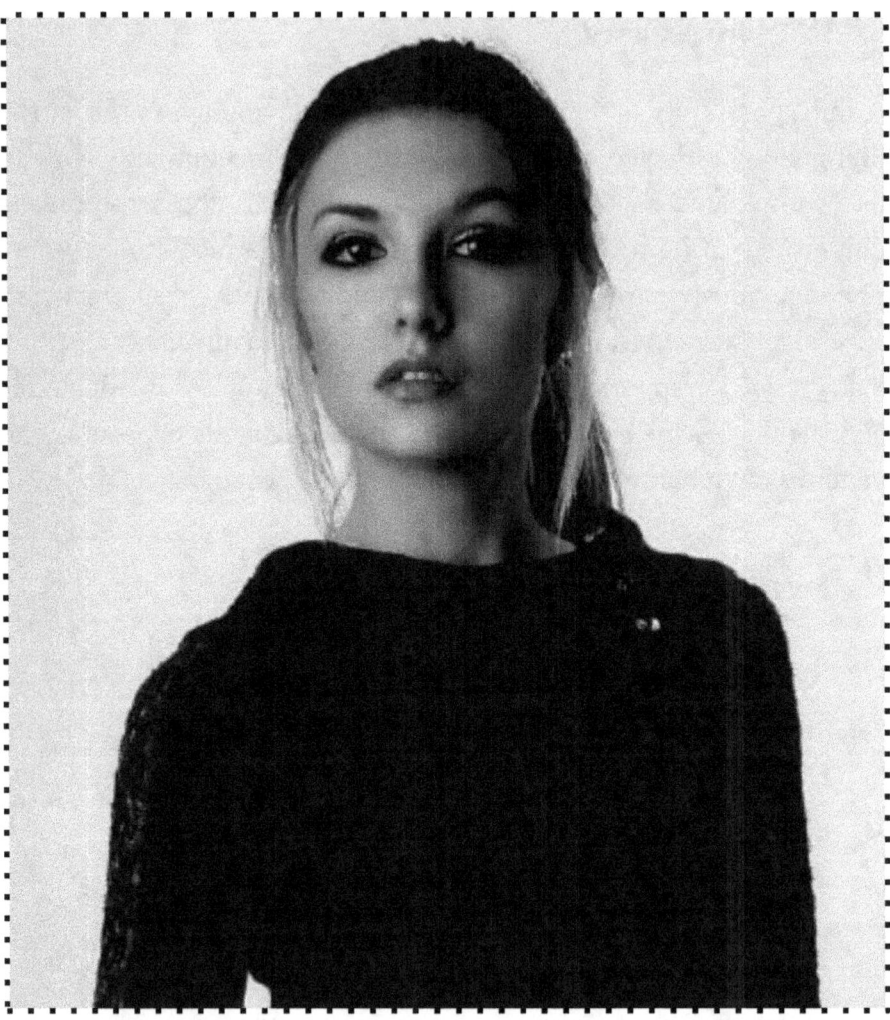

Thereafter, there are four approaches to selecting the proper aperture and shutter speed when utilizing the manual and semi-automatic shooting modes. Aperture-priority, Shutter-priority, Program, and Manual options are selectable by rotating the mode dial while depressing the mode dial release lever located on the upper-left shoulder of the camera. Your choice regarding which is optimal for a particular shooting scenario will be influenced by factors such as the amount of depth-of-field you require (or prefer), whether you prefer motion blur or freezing action, and the amount of noise you consider acceptable in an image. Below are the explanations of the four exposure methods;

Aperture-Priority

Aperture-priority (A) mode allows the user to designate the applied lens opening, with the camera subsequently adjusting the shutter speed to correspond with the aperture and ISO sensitivity being utilized. For instance, when the aperture is modified from f/5.6 to f/11, the camera will autonomously adjust the shutter speed to f/11 in order to preserve the identical exposure, relying on the input of the integrated light meter. Aperture-Priority is particularly advantageous when a specific lens opening is required to accomplish a desir

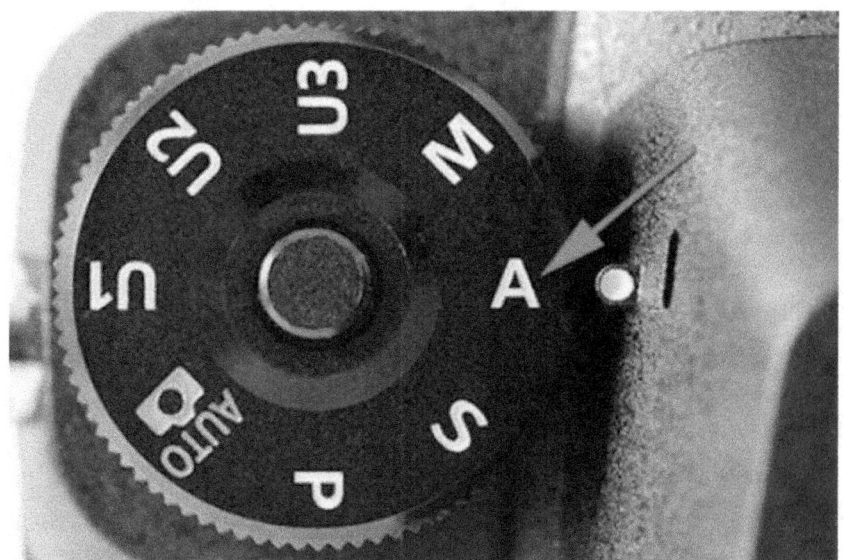

ed effect. For a close-up photograph, you might wish to utilize the smallest f/stop practicable (such as f/22) in order to maximize depth-of-field (DOF). Alternatively, you could employ a large f/stop to blur everything in the frame except the subject at hand. Perhaps you simply wish to "lock in" a specific f/stop because it corresponds to the lens's sharpest aperture. Another option would be to utilize an aperture of f/2.8 on a lens that has a maximal aperture of f/1.4, in order to achieve the optimal balance between shutter speed and image clarity.

Aperture priority can also be used to specify a range of shutter velocities to be employed in different illumination conditions. But note this; if you are using a telephoto lens to capture an outdoor soccer game and desire a shutter speed that is comparatively fast, but it is not a big deal if the speed slightly decreases if the sun disappears behind a cloud. At the current ISO setting, set the exposure method to A and modify the aperture until a shutter speed of, say, 1/1000 second is achieved. (At ISO 400 and in direct sunlight, the aperture is approximately f/11.) Proceed with the shooting, assured that your camera will retain the f/11 aperture (to capture depth-of-field adequately as the soccer players navigate the field), but will automatically reduce to 1/750th or 1/500th second if the illumination conditions slightly alter.

Going further, a blinking top-panel monochrome LCD and the shutter speed indicator in the viewfinder indicate that it is not possible to specify an appropriate shutter speed for the selected aperture, and that overexposure and underexposure will occur at the current ISO setting. A significant drawback of aperture priority is the possibility of selecting an f/stop that is either excessively small or large in comparison to the shutter speeds available, thereby preventing an optimal exposure. For instance, in situations where the illumination is extremely brilliant (e.g., at the seashore or in snow) and the aperture is set to f/2.8, the highest shutter speed on your camera may not be sufficient to reduce the quantity of light reaching the sensor in time to produce the desired exposure. Alternatively, if you choose f/8 in a dimly illuminated room, you may be forced to use an extremely sluggish shutter speed, which may result in distortion due to camera tremor or subject motion. Aperture priority is most effectively utilized by those who have some experience selecting settings. Numerous experienced photographers always leave their camera set to A. Indicating the degree of underexposure or overexposure, the control panel and viewfinder feature an exposure indicator scale. The image below illustrates the application of Aperture Priority in photography:

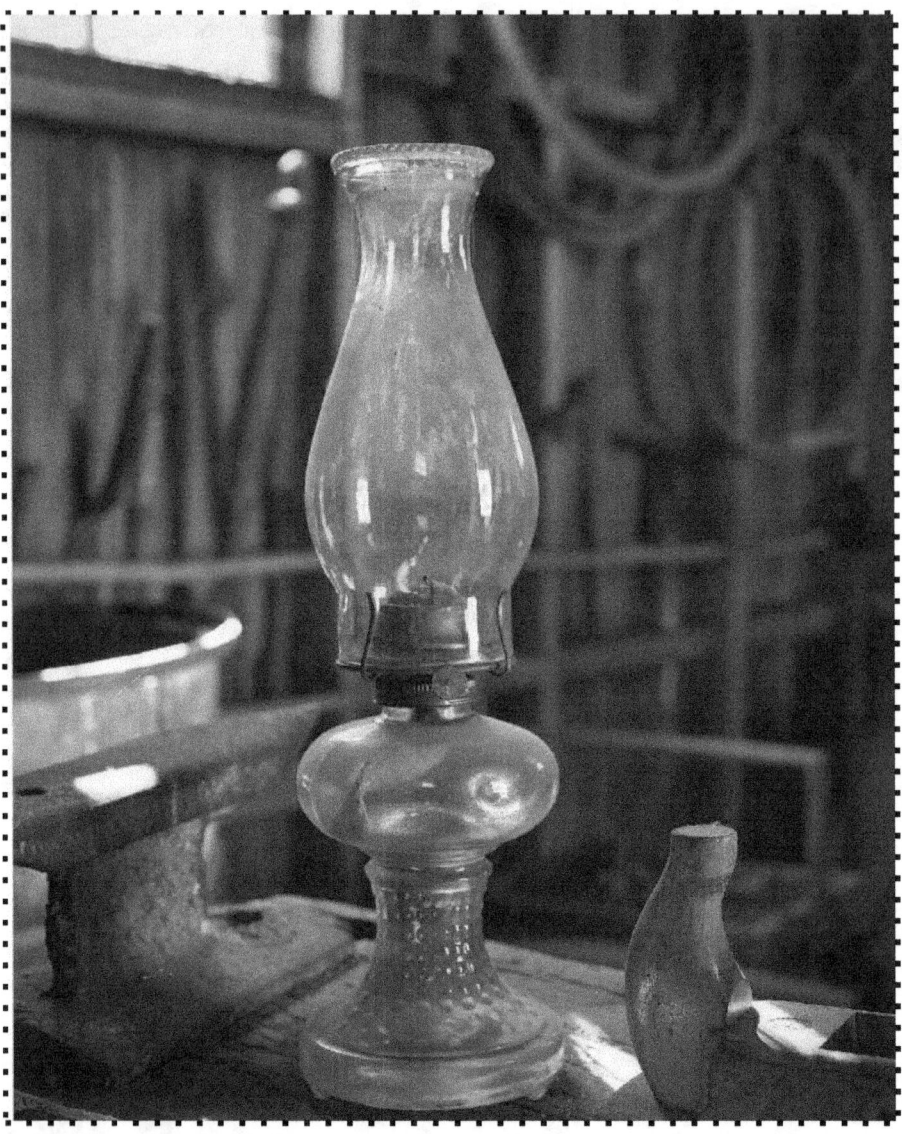

The following are instances and scenarios in which the Aperture Priority Mode can be utilized:

1. Shooting in general Landscape photography: Obviously, the z8 is an exceptional camera for landscape photography due to the fact that its high resolution enables the creation of both colossal, aesthetically pleasing photographs and smaller ones brimming with astounding detail. Aperture priority is a useful setting for achieving sharpness across the entire landscape, from the foreground to infinity, provided that the f/stop chosen maximizes the depth of field. When utilizing Aperture-priority mode and choosing an aperture such as f/11 or f/16, it becomes your duty to ensure that the shutter speed is sufficiently quick to prevent detail loss due to camera motion, or alternatively, to secure the camera to a tripod. An aspect that novice landscape photographers often overlook is the potential motion of distant tree branches and foliage. When aiming for maximum resolution, utilize aperture priority; however, if necessary, increase ISO sensitivity slightly to ensure an adequate shutter speed when photographing handheld or with a tripod.

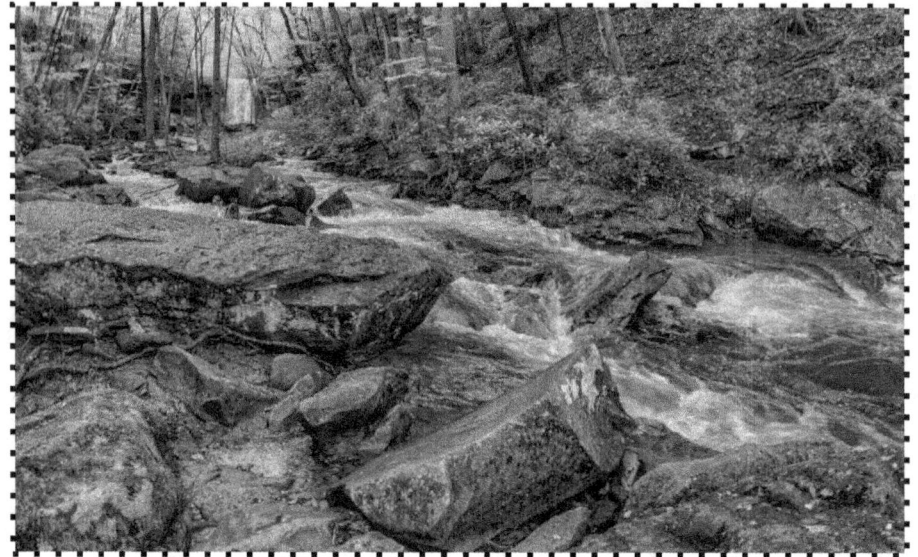

2. Exceptional Landscape photography: In certain landscape scenarios, aperture priority can be advantageous, especially when there are no objections to employing a lengthy shutter speed or when you specifically desire the camera to choose one. Such are waterfalls as an illustration. By employing aperture-priority mode, adjusting the camera's setting to ISO 100, utilizing a small f/stop, and allowing the exposure system to determine an extended shutter speed, one can achieve a blurred image of the flowing water. In fact, a neutral-density filter may be required to achieve an adequate shutter speed. However, aperture priority mode serves as a satisfactory initial step.

3. Shooting Portraits: This mode is often applied, when combined with an extended lens or zoom setting (in the 85mm–135mm range) and a medium-large aperture (e.g.,

f/5.6 or f/8), the background behind the subject of your portrait will become blurred. A very large aperture permits selective focus on the visage of the subject. As long as the subject's eyes remain keen and observed from a three-quarters angle, it is acceptable for the distant ear or hair to be out of focus.

4. When you want to achieve the highest level of focus: Every lens possesses one or two apertures at which it operates optimally, delivering the grade of clarity that you anticipate. Typically, this is two stops below the lens's widest aperture; however, this value can differ based on the lens's utmost aperture.

5. Macro/ close-up photography: When photographing macro subjects, depth-of-field is typically quite shallow; therefore, f/stop selection is crucial. It is possible that a wider pause could be utilized to accentuate the subject. Alternatively, to optimize depth-of-field, you might require the smallest aperture on your device. Additionally, aperture-priority mode is an invaluable tool when capturing close-up images. Because macro work is frequently accomplished with a tripod-mounted camera and close-up subjects, if not living organisms, may not be in motion significantly, a prolonged shutter speed is not an issue. Priority of the aperture may be the preferable option.

Shutter-Priority

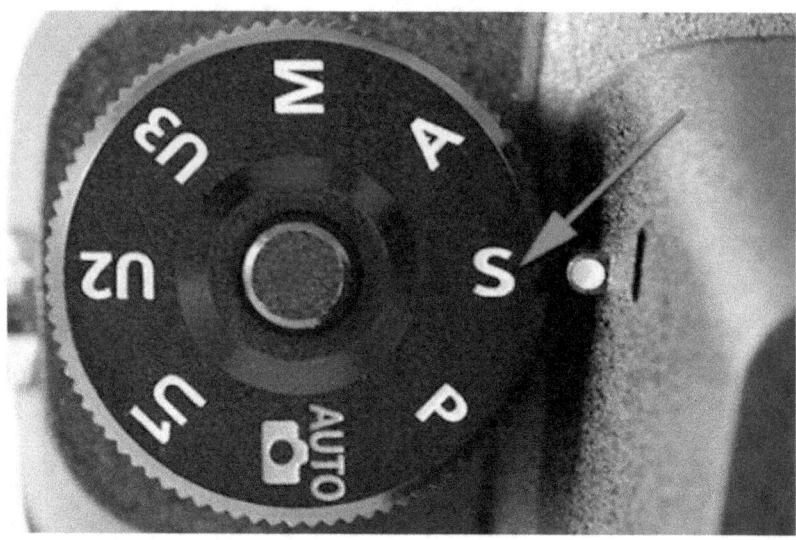

Shutter-priority (S) is the antithesis of aperture-priority: the metering system determines the appropriate f/stop based on the shutter speed you specify. Sometimes, you may desire to use the quickest shutter speed possible when capturing action photographs; other times, you might wish to add some motion to an action photograph that would be unremarkable if the action were completely halted by employing a slower shutter speed. You have some influence over the extent to which your digital camera's action-freezing capabilities are utilized in a given situation by utilizing the shutter priority mode.

Note; caution is advised when employing a slow shutter speed of 1/8 second or less, as camera motion will cause distortion unless vibration reduction is utilized or the camera is mounted on a tripod or other stable support. Similarly to aperture priority, you will face the same issue when choosing a shutter speed that is either too lengthy or too brief for proper exposure in certain circumstances. Similar to aperture priority mode, an undesirable shutter speed can be selected. The shutter speed indicator in the viewfinder and control panel LCD will flicker if this is the case. The following are examples of when shutter-priority can be used:

1. To reduce blur from subject motion: An effective method for mitigating distortion caused by moving subjects is to increase the shutter speed. The precise pace will differ based on the subject's velocity and the desired level of distortion. To add a sense of motion, you might use a 1/200th second shutter speed to enable the rotating wheels of a motocross racer to distort slightly, or 1/1000th second to capture a basketball player in mid-dunk.

2. To add blur from subject motion: There are circumstances in which blurring a subject is desirable, such as when utilizing Shutter-priority mode to capture cascades with a one- to two-second exposure.

3. To add blur from camera motion when you are moving: For example, if you are planning to enable you shoot some relay sprinters. It is possible that by setting the shutter speed to 1/60 second in shutter priority mode, the background will become less distinct while you pan with the runners. The shutter speed will be sufficient to render the athletes in precise focus while blurring their obtrusive background. The image below demonstrates how shutter priority can be utilized to designate a shutter speed that produces a fairly clear image of a moving subject.

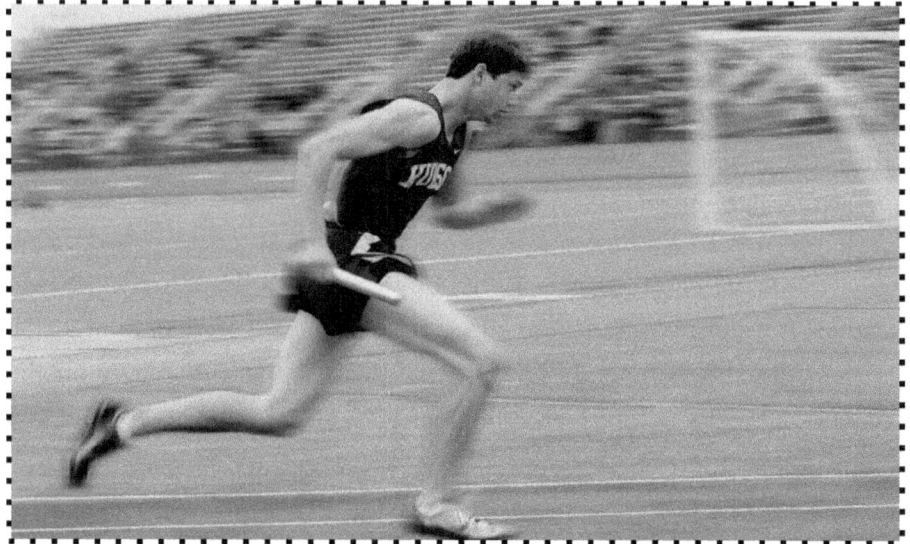

4. To reduce blur caused as a result of moving or shaking the camera: There are instance where your camera will be in motion which makes it unstable, for example, if you are photographing from a moving train or automobile; if you wish to minimize blur caused by camera motion, the shutter priority mode is an excellent option.

5. Landscape photography hand-held: For example, if you are shooting in landscape, particularly when you are capturing scenes where surges of wind may cause foliage to flutter without a tripod, you can still shoot a perfect image. The Shutter-priority helps you to specify a shutter speed that is quick enough to reduce or eliminate the effects of camera motion. However, ensure that the ISO setting is sufficiently high to enable the camera to choose an aperture that provides adequate depth-of-field.

6. Concerts and stage performances: It is recommended to utilize the 70-200mm f/2.8 VR Nikkor lens in conjunction with the FTZ adapter when shooting in this scenario. Also, a shutter speed of 1/180 second is sufficient. Additionally, vibration reduction is necessary to eliminate camera shake that will occur when holding the camera by hand while using this lens, and to prevent blur that will occur as result of the steady movement of the stage performers.

Program Mode

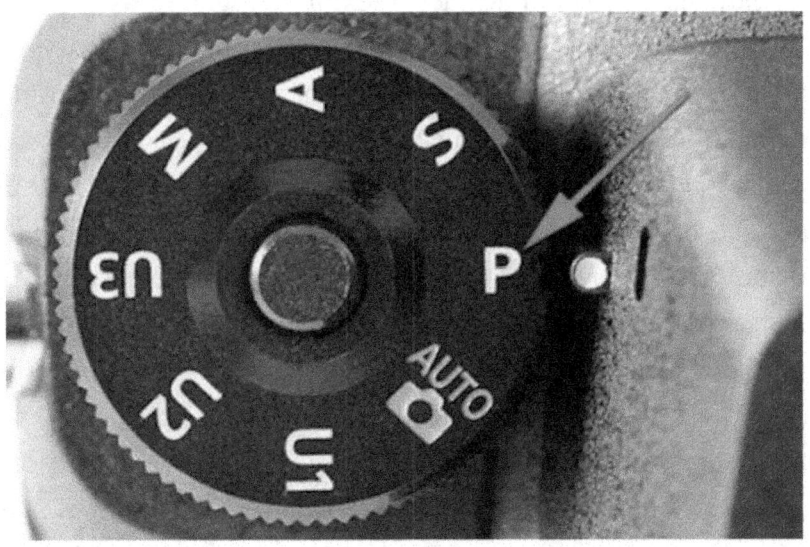

Program mode (P) employs the camera's integrated intelligence to determine the optimal f/stop and shutter speed for a given image by consulting a database containing picture data that specifies the optimal combination of aperture and shutter speed. When the current ISO setting fails to produce the intended exposure, the shutter speed and aperture will exhibit blinking indicators in both the viewfinder and control panel. The ISO can subsequently be increased or decreased in order to adjust the sensitivity.

By manipulating the EV (exposure value) setting, one can augment or diminish the measured exposure value. It should be noted that while in Program mode, it is possible to alter the recommended setting by rotating the main command dial to access the equivalent setting. This setting yields an identical exposure, albeit with a distinct combination of f/stop and shutter speed.

Nikon calls the Program Mode "Flexible Program" as well. By rotating the main command dial to the left, the aperture can be decreased from f/4 to f/5.6. This adjustment will result in the camera automatically employing a reduced shutter speed, specifically from 1/200th second to 1/125th second. By rotating the main command dial to the right, one can employ a larger f/stop while having the shutter speed automatically reduced to achieve an equivalent exposure that is identical to that measured in P mode. If you see an asterisk sign appear next to the letter P in the viewfinder or monitor, it means the preset program setting has been overridden. Until you rotate the main command dial which causes the asterisk to disappear, even though you change the exposure mode, or power off the camera, your adjustment will remain in effect.

Occasionally, the desired level of exposure may differ from what the metering system indicates. You might wish to underexpose for a silhouette effect or overexpose for a high-key appearance. Overriding the exposure recommendations is a simple process using the exposure compensation mechanism of the camera. In order to initiate exposure compensation (EV), locate the button just southeast of the shutter release on the upper panel. To add exposure, turn the main command dial to the left; to subtract exposure, turn it to the right. The EV adjustment that you have performed persists for subsequent exposures, unless you manually reset the EV setting to zero. In the control panel and viewfinder, the EV plus/minus icon indicates when an exposure compensation adjustment has been made. Moreso, activating Easy Exposure Compensation via Custom Setting b2 eliminates the need to depress the EV button when using Program, Aperture-priority, Shutter-priority, or Manual exposure modes; the EV value can be adjusted by rotating the main or sub-command dials exclusively. The following are instances where you can utilize this mode (Program mode):

1. When you want to take a shot immediately: The camera will calculate an appropriate exposure for you with reasonable accuracy, even in the absence of your input.

2. When the shot is to be taken by a novice: Place the camera on P and give control of the camera to the novice. The camera will calculate the appropriate exposure.

3. In situations where aperture and shutter speed adjustments are unnecessary: Utilize P as a general-purpose setting if your subject does not necessitate any specific anti-blur or selective focus techniques, and depth-of-field or selective focus are not important. Note; you can make simple adjustments in order to augment or reduce motion blur or depth of field.

Manual Exposure

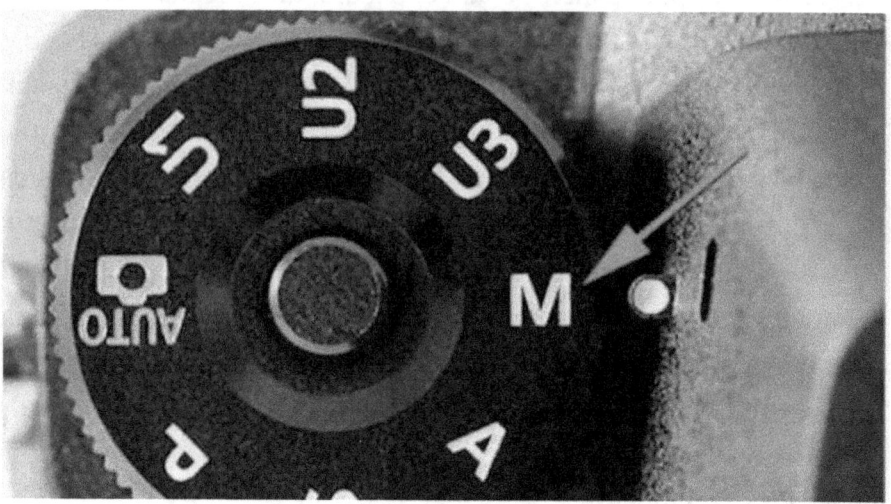

Proficiency in photography includes the ability to discern when to utilize the automation features of the camera (P mode), when to employ semi-automatic exposure settings (S or A), and when to manually adjust exposure (M mode). Certain photographers may even prefer to set their exposure manually, as the analog exposure scale at the bottom of the viewfinder will indicate when the camera's metering system determines that the manual settings produce the desired exposure.

Manual exposure can be advantageous in certain circumstances. For example, while attempting to capture a silhouette, you will discover that none of the exposure modes or EV correction functions produce the desired effect; manually adjust the exposure to achieve the precise shutter speed and f/stop required. This mode is important if you operate multiple flash devices in a studio environment. External devices (gadgets that activate the flash when they detect light from another flash unit, or potentially from a radio or infrared remote control) are responsible for activating the additional flashes. In the absence of exposure meter compensation for the additional illumination, manual aperture adjustment is required.

Although, your personal inclinations may not necessitate often setting exposure manually, it is still advisable to possess a comprehensive understanding of its operation. Thankfully, the camera makes manually adjusting the exposure extremely simple. To enter Manual mode, simply disengage the lock on the mode dial and rotate it to the M position. To modify the aperture and shutter speed, utilize the sub-command dial and the primary command dial, respectively. By halfway depressing the shutter release or activating the designated AE lock button, the exposure scale displayed in the viewfinder will indicate the degree of deviation between the selected setting and the metered exposure.

It should be noted that; older lenses lacking the CPU processor responsible for identifying the type of lens affixed on the camera can only be utilized in aperture-priority and manual exposure modes, that is if you have provided the Non-CPU Lens information in the Setup menu. Once the camera is aware of the lens's maximum aperture, the aperture can be adjusted via the aperture ring of the lens. When the camera is operating in aperture-priority mode, it will determine an appropriate shutter speed automatically. The aperture can be adjusted in Manual mode, and the analog exposure scale displayed in the viewfinder will indicate when the appropriate shutter speed has been manually set. The following are instances in which manual exposure should be utilized:

1. When shooting in the studio: When operating within a studio area, you typically possess absolute authority over the lighting conditions and can precisely adjust the exposure. The last thing you need is for the camera to autonomously interpret and adapt the scene. Utilize the M mode; this is because the shutter speed, aperture, and ISO setting are entirely up to you (as long as you avoid using ISO Auto).

2. When employing standard flash: The Nikon Creative Lighting System (CLS) and the newly introduced Advanced Lighting System (ALS, which debuted with the SB-5000) are both noteworthy innovations. Moreover, they enable seamless coordination between the camera and external dedicated flash units that are compatible with the SB-910 or SB-5000. However, when utilizing non-CLS flash units, specifically studio flashes connected to the PC/X flash adapter, the camera is oblivious to the flash's intensity; therefore, you must manually adjust the aperture.

3. If you're using a hand-held light meter: The appropriate aperture for both flash exposures and photos captured under continuous lighting can be determined using a hand-held light meter, flash meter, or combi meter, which is capable of measuring both types of illumination. By employing an external meter, you are capable of independently measuring highlights, shadows, backgrounds, or supplementary subjects, and subsequently adjusting the exposure manually.

4. In order to circumvent the metering system: Backlighting, abnormally intense illumination, or low-key images with

indistinct shadows are examples of circumstances in which your metering system has been "trained" to respond to. It is often capable of overcoming these "problems" and producing well-exposed images. Manual exposure enables you to create silhouettes in backlit situations, eliminate all intermediate tones for a luminous effect, or underexpose for a gloomy or ominous dark-toned photograph, all without achieving a well-exposed image.

5. When you want to select aperture and shutter speed: Aperture and shutter priority provide auto exposure while enabling you to set in an aperture or shutter speed of your choosing—but not both simultaneously. Manual exposure permits the specification of both while preserving auto exposure capabilities. Simply go about activating ISO Auto. While maintaining the desired shutter speed and aperture, the camera will adjust the sensitivity to achieve the desired exposure.

6. When you want extra-long exposures: When you want extra-long exposures, none of the semi-automatic modes will produce anything beyond a 30-second exposure. In Manual mode, however, it is possible to extend exposure times to a maximum of 30 seconds by rotating the command dial to Time or Bulb. The extended exposure function, which permits timed photos of up to 900 seconds in Manual exposure mode, simplifies and improves the precision of such lengthy exposures. The image below is an illustration of a shot with an extra-long exposure.

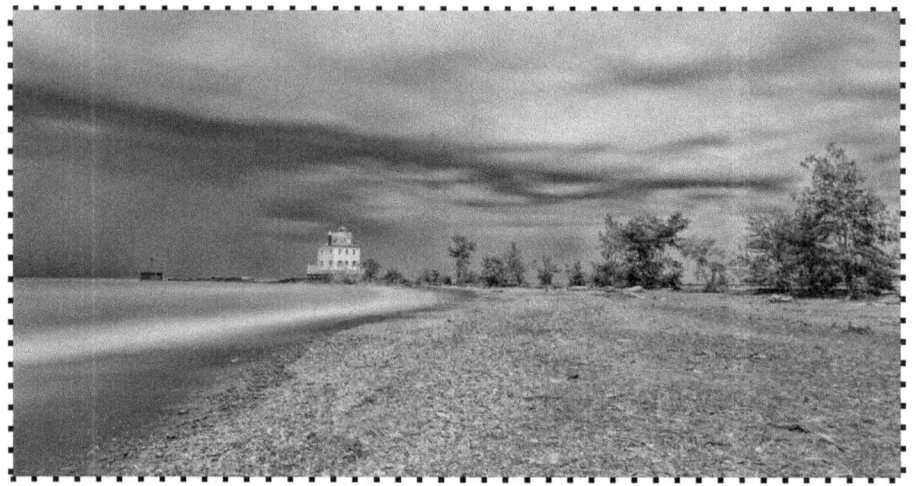

Adjusting Exposure with ISO Settings

An alternative method of manipulating exposures involves altering the ISO sensitivity setting. As it is common practice for photographers to set the ISO once for a specific photography session (for instance, to 800 for indoors or 200 for intense sunlight outdoors) and then forget about it, this option is occasionally overlooked. ISOs exceeding 200 or 400 are considered "evil" or "necessary." Nevertheless, modifying the ISO is a standard method of altering exposure settings, especially with cameras such as the z8, which yields satisfactory outcomes at ISO settings where other models produce unusable, pixelated images.

ISO adjustment serves as a practical alternative method for adjusting exposure values by adding or subtracting EV when operating in Manual mode. Additionally, it facilitates the selection of equivalent exposures when in Program, Shutter-priority, or Aperture-priority modes. For instance, suppose you have chosen an ISO 200 manual exposure setting with an appropriate f/stop and shutter speed for my image. By rotating the main command dial one click at a time while holding down the ISO button located on the top-right shoulder of the camera, the exposure can be adjusted in 1/3-stop increments. Although adjusting the exposure slightly to ISO 160 or ISO 125 will result in negligible image quality and noise reduction, doing the same with ISO 250 or 320 will substantially increase exposure. While retaining the desired f/stop and shutter speed, it is possible to modify the exposure. Additionally, keep in mind that when ISO Auto is engaged, you can instruct the camera to autonomously establish the exposure using the desired f/stop and shutter speed.

Additionally, if shutter priority mode is employed and the measured exposure at ISO 200 is 1/500 second at f/11. However, if you decide that that 1/500 second at f/8 is more suitable, you can change the ISO setting by pressing the ISO button and turning the main command dial to ISO 100. Recommendably, it is best to monitor your ISO adjustments in order to avoid inadvertently reaching ISO 6400. In both the control panel and the viewfinder, an ISO indicator serves as a visual reminder of the dialed sensitivity setting.

The ISO parameters can also be utilized to increase or decrease sensitivity in specific shooting situations. In addition to standard ISO settings ranging from ISO 64 to ISO 25,600, the z8 features "extended" Lo and Hi settings extending to Lo 1 (equivalent to ISO 32) and Hi 2, respectively (equivalent to ISO 102,400). The 24MP resolution of the z8 provides an alternative sensitivity range. It includes extended ISO settings from Lo 1 (equivalent to ISO 50) to Hi 2 (equivalent to ISO 204,800) in addition to standard ISO settings from ISO 100 to ISO 51,200. Additionally, the camera is capable of autonomously adjusting the ISO to compensate for different lighting conditions. When the Auto ISO option is selected from the Photo Shooting menu, the camera dynamically adjusts the sensitivity to the subject matter in accordance with the minimal shutter speed and ISO limits that the user specifies. It is important to exercise caution when utilizing Auto ISO, as it can cause the camera to employ an ISO value that is higher than what you would have chosen otherwise.

Several advantageous features are included in the camera's Auto ISO arsenal. For example, by identifying limits and specifying a maximal sensitivity, the camera will never choose an ISO that you consider to be excessively high. Furthermore, should the exposure yield a shutter speed that is slower than the minimum you specify (thus exposing the image to distortion caused by subject motion or camera movement), the camera will automatically adjust to a higher ISO setting in order to enable the use of the minimum shutter speed or quicker.

ABOUT THE CAMERA METERING MID-TONES

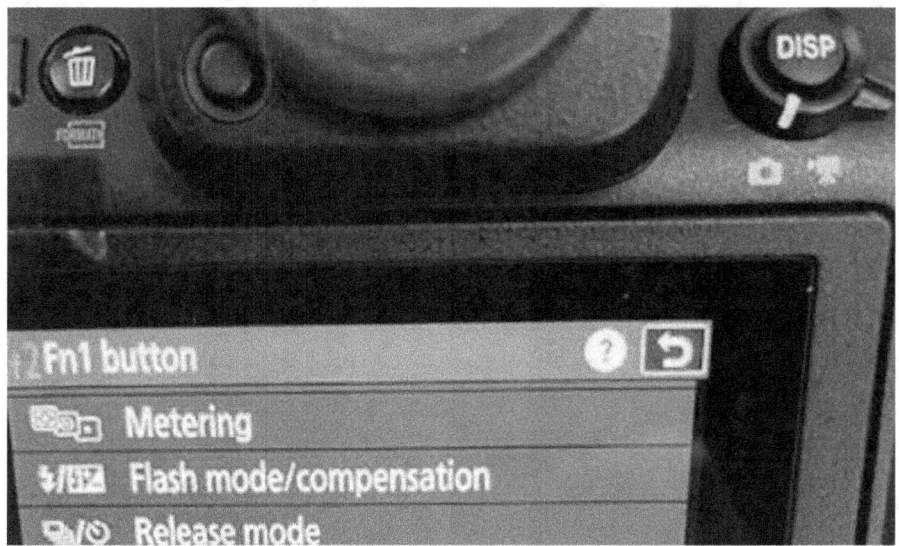

As previously mentioned, the most accurate method for determining exposure is to use a meter against a subject that reflects between 12 and 18 percent of the incident light. To achieve the most accurate exposure calculations, a substitute must be utilized. Also, a rich, medium-blue sky or any midtone subject, such as verdant vegetation, reflects between 12 and 18 percent of the incident light. By calibrating this region, the overall exposure of the scene can be guaranteed to be accurate or nearly accurate for subjects of average stature.

Certain extremely dazzling scenes (such as a volcanic field or a wintry landscape) will lack a midtone to meter. The palm of a human hand can also be used as an alternative to a gray card, since the back of the hand is too variable. However, a human palm is even sharper than a standard gray card; therefore, one additional stop of exposure is required as opposed to the half stop. In other words, utilize 1/500th

83

second at f/8 or 1/200th second at f/11 in lieu of the 1/500th of a second reading from your meter at f/11. Equal exposures apply to both. Alternatively, one could utilize the gray card that was previously mentioned and illuminated uniformly. There are compact variants that are suitable for carrying in a camera case. Position it in the frame in close proximity to the primary subject, with its face facing the camera and under the same even illumination that is raining on the subject. Subsequently, compute the exposure using the Spot metering function. However, the standard Kodak gray card reflects 18 percent of the light, whereas your camera is calibrated for a slightly darker 12 percent tone. Should you desire to achieve an ideal exposure, it would be necessary to incorporate an additional half stop of exposure beyond the value indicated on the light meter card.

Choosing a Metering Method

The light received by the exposure sensors of the camera is evaluated using one of four schemes: matrix, center-weighted, spot, or highlight-weighted. Choose the desired mode from the i menu; alternatively, Custom Setting f2 can be used to designate the metering adjustment function to a custom control.

Please note; if you regularly utilize one metering method but sometimes you do change to another method spontaneously, you can redefine or reassign the Fn1 or Fn2 controls on the camera to instantaneously transition to your preferred mode. Using Custom Setting f2, the buttons will be programmed to deliver matrix-weighted, center-weighted, spot-weighted, or highlight-weighted illumination. One noteworthy aspect is that it is possible to designate a button for Spot metering and another for Center-weighted metering.

Furthermore, the metering mode switch can be set to Matrix, allowing for effortless switching between the aforementioned three modes. It is worth noting that the indicators displayed in the viewfinder can assist in recalling the metering mode that has been selected. The symbol for each metering mode is represented in the image below.

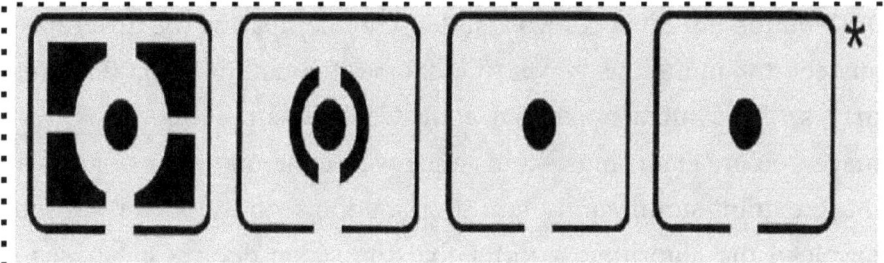

By analyzing the light that passes through the lens and impacts the sensor, your camera determines exposure. At ISO 100, these particles are reportedly capable of detecting light within the range of -3 to $+17$ EV. This corresponds to an increase in exposure time from eight minutes at f/16 to 1/1000 second at f/16.

From a practical standpoint, the illumination outside during the night under a full moon is denoted by 0 EV, whereas the brightest scene of the day (snow in broad daylight) is approximately 16 EV. Your camera is capable of detecting photons across an exceptionally broad EV range, which is one stop brighter than daylight snow and two stops dimmer than full moonlight. Nevertheless, the capacity to capture images is significantly constrained in scope. It should be noted that the dynamic range of the sensor, which refers to the tones it can retain in the final image, is smaller than the complete range of tones that it is capable of detecting.

Matrix Metering

In matrix metering mode, the camera compares the luminance of numerous areas using a matrix array to the light descending on the sensor. A symbol indicator is displayed on the photo information screen when matrix metering is active; to access it, tap and hold the DISP button until it becomes visible. After comparing the differences between the numerous zones to a database containing 30,000 actual images, the camera makes an educated estimate as to the type of image you are capturing. An instance where the upper portions of an image exhibit significantly less illumination than the lower portions may lead the algorithm to infer that the scene depicts a landscape photograph replete with sky. However, if the camera detects skin tones in a lighter area in the center of the frame, it will expose for the human subject and presume you are photographing a portrait rather than a landscape. The following is an illustration of matrix metering:

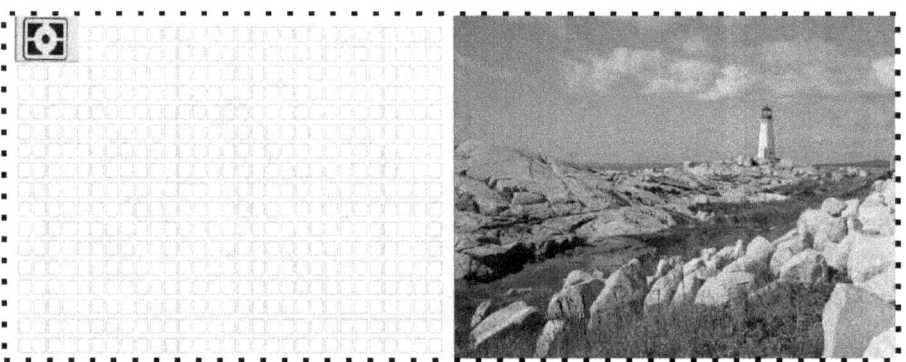

Note; the Matrix Metering symbol is often shown in the upper left corner of the display. Matrix metering mode can frequently identify a wide variety of light scenes and increase the exposure automatically to prevent the capture of gloomy images. For example, when your subject is a snow-covered landscape or a close-up of a bride in white, this will be useful. Although it may be necessary to apply some exposure compensation on occasion, the exposure is frequently accurate enough to be considered adequate without it. Matrix metering is the most effective when applied to bright-day scenes with mild tones and when humans are present in the frame. Most likely, you will get an underexposed scene when photographing in overcast and dim conditions, with this metering mode.

Moreover, exposure meters have historically computed accurate exposure based on luminance. The sophisticated exposure technology incorporates additional data to generate more intelligent settings. These factors consist of:

1. Patterns: By comparing the exposure of each pixel on the sensor to a database containing tens of thousands of image types, the camera searches for pixel-level differences and database-level similarities. Upon identifying a match, the system utilizes that data to generate a suggested exposure. When the contrast of a scene reaches a level where the sensor is unlikely to retain detail in both shadows and highlights, the camera will typically prioritize the highlights. Highlights are irretrievably erased; however, data may occasionally be recoverable from shadow regions. When recording RAW, alterations to the exposure and other parameters can frequently amplify details in darkened regions.

2. Colors: The camera is capable of improving its readings by detecting and analyzing the colors present in the frame. Significant expanses of blue in the upper portion of the image

can be identified as the sky; the presence of skin tones strongly suggests the presence of human beings; and the greens can be reasonably interpreted as foliage.

3. Autofocus region: Regardless of whether the autofocus zone is selected by the user or the camera, the exposure system logically implies that the in-focus portion of the image contains the subject.

4. Aspect ratio and focal length: The distance and focal length provided by your Z-mount lenses are utilized to determine the nature of the scene you have captured more precisely. For example, when capturing a portrait using a lens of extended focal length and focusing to a distance of 5 to 12 feet from the subject, and the upper portion of the scene exhibits intense brightness, the camera will disregard the bright area in anticipation that the subject wishes to meter the remainder of the image. Nevertheless, by attaching a wide-angle lens and focusing it at infinity, the camera can detect that you are capturing a landscape image and adjust the appearance of the sky and clouds to compensate for the brilliant upper portion.

Due to its ability to analytically analyze a scene and make an excellent estimate as to what kind of subject you are photographing the most of the time, matrix metering is ideal for the majority of general subjects. The camera is capable of distinguishing between subjects with low contrast and those with high contrast by analyzing the spectrum of luminance variations present in the scene. When image contrast is high and the camera has a reasonable understanding of the subject matter being captured, it may underexpose slightly in order to preserve highlight detail.

Note; It is recommended to switch from Matrix metering to Center-weighted when employing a strong filter, such as a graduated neutral-density filter, polarizing filter, split-color filter, or neutral-density filter (especially a graduated neutral-density filter). This is due to the potential impact that the filter may have on the interrelationships among the various frame regions utilized in the Matrix exposure calculation. For example, the application of a polarizing filter results in an abnormally dark sky, which impedes the Matrix algorithm's ability to identify a landscape photograph. Colored or extremely dark filters disrupt the color relationships that are utilized in color matrix metering.

Center-weighted Metering

To compute exposure in this mode, the exposure meter accentuates a 12mm zone in the center of the frame. Several years ago, this particular metering method was the sole option and was regarded as an improvement over averaging, which calculated exposure by summing the illumination of the entire frame. Center-weighted metering yields traditional metering without incorporating any "intelligent" scene assessment. The light meter takes into account the overall luminance of the frame, but prioritizes a significant region in the center, operating under the assumption that the primary subject will not be significantly off-center in the majority of photographs.

Approximately 75% of the exposure is determined by the 12mm central area that was selected, while the remaining 25% is determined by the remainder of the frame. Therefore, in the event that the camera detects the center portion and ascertains that it requires an exposure of f/4 at 1/250 second, while the outer region, which is slightly darker, requires f/16 at 1/250 second, it will prioritize the center portion and calculate a final exposure of approximately f/5.6 at 1/250 second.

Effective use of center-weighted metering requires a midtone subject in the central area. Notwithstanding this, the exposure may not be ideal if the focal point is encompassed by expansive, exceedingly brilliant or gloomy regions. This setting is beneficial for photographing portraits or close-ups of subjects such as flowers. One option is to utilize the default 12mm circle, while the alternative is to select "Average" (which effectively encompasses the entire screen and generates average measurements

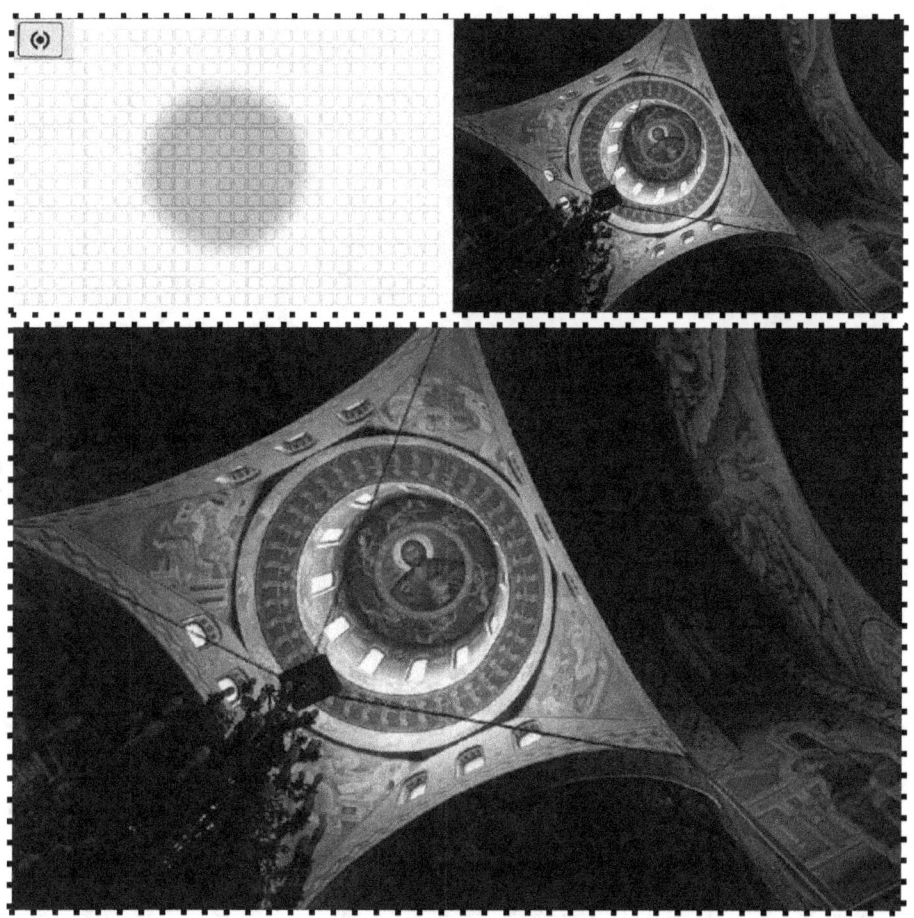

Spot Metering

Individuals who have utilized a handheld light meter to assess exposure at different locations (e.g., separately metering highlights and shadows) tend to prefer spot metering. Nevertheless, spot metering can be employed in any circumstance wherein one desires to precisely quantify the light that is reflected from light, midtone, dark, or any combination thereof, regions of the subject.

91

This mode restricts the viewing area in the viewfinder to a restricted 4mm region, comprising a mere 1.5 percent of the screen. It is important to note that while the circle is centered on the active focus point (which is not limited to the one depicted in the figure), it is larger than the focus point itself. This distinction should not mislead one into believing that exposure measurement is limited to the viewfinder indicators that symbolize the active focus point. This is the only method of metering that permits precise location of exposure measurement within the frame. The spot meter, on the other hand, utilizes solely the center focus point when Auto-area AF is enabled.

Spot metering is a valuable tool for determining exposure for a specific region within a given frame. It is preferable if that area is positioned in the center of the frame. If this is not the case, you will need to use an appropriate focus point to obtain a meter reading for an off-center subject, and then secure exposure by halfway depressing the shutter release button or by tapping the center of the sub-selector. This mode is most effective when the background is considerably darker or livelier than the subject.

Spot metering a region with extremely light or dark tones will result in underexposure or overexposure, respectively; for more precise readings, an override is required. Conversely, a decent exposure can be obtained by spot metering a small midtone subject surrounded by a sky filled with large white clouds or by an indigo blue wall.

In essence, matrix and center-weighted metering offer limited alternatives for consideration. Both are only impacted by making adjustments to Custom Setting b4: Fine-Tune Optimal Exposure and exposure compensation. Conversely, spot metering can be enhanced by your involvement in the selection process of the location. The following are several factors to bear in mind:

1. Shifting the spot: It is important to note that when you adjust the spot, the current focal spot remains in effect. Therefore, you must be utilizing an AF-area mode that permits the modification of the AF spot, which is any AF-area mode besides Auto-area AF, which utilizes the center focus point as the metering spot at all times and cannot be modified.

2. Selecting a compatible AF-area mode: To navigate through the available AF areas, which vary based on the selected focus mode, utilize the i menu. By utilizing any of the following AF-area configurations, the AF point can be moved to any of the focus areas that are displayed:

93

- Wide-area AF (Small), Wide-area AF (Large), Pinpoint AF, or Wide-area AF (Small) are the AF-S focus modes. (Please note that dynamic-area AF is not offered.)

- Single-point AF, Dynamic-area AF, Wide-area AF (Small), or Wide-area AF (Large) comprise the AF-C focus mode. (Please note that Pinpoint AF is not offered.)

- Manual focus mode restricts the user to selecting a single point. It should be noted that the camera does not automatically focus when manual focus is applied. The focus point position is exclusively utilized for the electronic rangefinder and spot metering capabilities.

3. Wrap around: Utilize the directional controls on the multi-selector or the sub-selector to rotate the AF point and the metering area within the display. The movement of the focus point will cease at the left, right, top, and bottom boundaries unless focus point wrap-around is enabled in Custom Setting a8.

4. When using Auto-area AF: When Auto-area AF is enabled, the center focus point will consistently be utilized, notwithstanding the camera's choice of an alternative point for the autofocus operation. This is actually a benefit: since the focus point remains unknown until you halfway press the shutter release button in Auto-area AF mode, it is reassuring to know that the camera will use the center location. Although spot metering is most effective when auto-area AF is not in use, it continues to operate albeit with reduced flexibility.

Note that the spot metering point also moves in tandem with the focus point. When Dynamic-area AF and continuous autofocus are employed, the camera may shift the initially selected focus point and refocus on the focus points in the surrounding area. Note; Metering area will follow suit. The image below serves as a practical example of Spot Metering in action against an extremely dark backdrop.

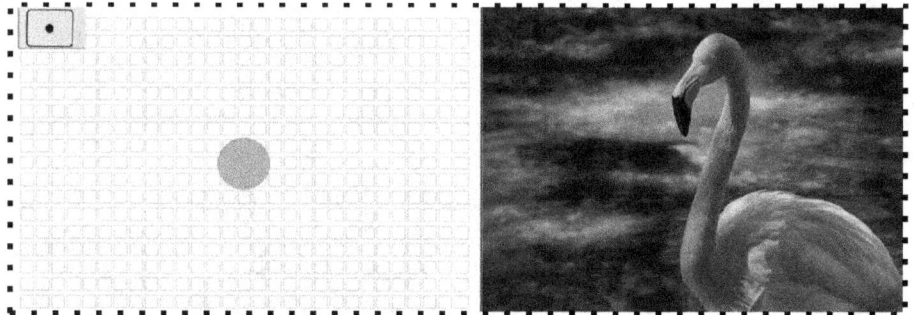

Highlight-weighted Metering

The exposure system examines the entire scene in this metering mode, just as it does when employing matrix metering. Although it shares the Spot icon with the addition of an asterisk, this mode does not utilize spot metering. In this mode, the dual Expeed 6 processors identify areas of your image that are highlighted and adjust the exposure to prevent those areas from being overexposed. Non-highlight regions are assigned to less prominence ("weight"). Nevertheless, keep in mind that highlight-weighted is more appropriate for images where the highlights are distributed across a more substantial portion of the frame. Therefore, when photographing spotlit performers onstage during a performance or concert, the camera can determine the appropriate exposure based on the performers themselves, disregarding the predominantly dim surroundings. As described in the preceding section, you could select Spot mode to determine exposure by positioning the metering spot on the face or shirt of the dancer. Alternatively, you could opt for Highlight-weighted metering, which would enable the camera to identify the performer for the purpose of determining exposure. The degree to which the system distinguishes your subject from the background and how precisely you "placed" the Spot area may influence whether your results are comparable with the other option. An example where the highlight weighted metering can be applied is during theatrical performance.

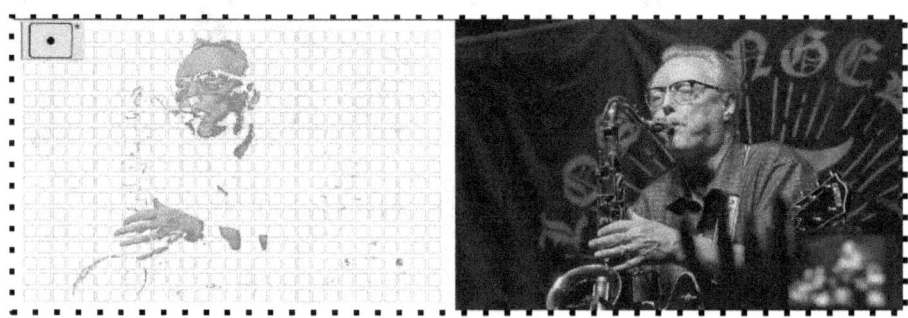

Once shutter speed, aperture, and ISO have been adjusted to your liking, the ability to secure exposure is a crucial feature when employing any metering method; it enables one to reframe the image prior to capturing it. By default, the sub-selector center button secures exposure and autofocus with the AE-L/AF-L configuration. However, using Custom Setting f2: Custom Controls, you can define an alternative control, such as the AF-ON button, for that function.

The control that is defined has the capability to operate as either an AE/AF lock or an AE Lock Only. The latter option proves to be advantageous when employing back-button focus, which will be elaborated upon in the following chapter. A Shutter Speed and Aperture Lock button, which effectively secures exposure by locking the shutter speed in aperture-priority mode and aperture in shutter-priority mode, can be defined using the identical custom setting.

Dealing with Noise

Visual image noise is that granular, random effect that some people enjoy using as a special effect, but which is generally undesirable because it detracts from the image's detail while adding an "interesting" texture. Noise arises from two distinct phenomena, namely extended exposure times and high ISO settings.

As the ISO setting is increased, the camera frequently produces high ISO noise. This is because the camera amplifies the base signal, which was captured at ISO 64 for the z8 and ISO 100 for the z8. An advancement observed in the camera is the integration of a dual gain signal amplifier. This feature enhances outcomes when employing higher ISO settings and, surprisingly, permits the preservation of superior contrast and image quality even when operating at sub-base ISO levels as low as Lo 1.

On the other hand, it is feasible to obtain images with comparatively minimal noise at ISO 800 and higher. However, some noise may become discernible at ISO 1600, and at ISO 6400 it is frequently quite apparent. At ISO 25,800 and higher, noise is frequently a significant nuisance; however, relatively low-contrast subjects can be captured at ISO 25,600. Nikon has recommended that settings exceeding ISO 25,600 will only be employed under exceptional conditions; these settings are designated Hi 0.3 through Hi 2. You will notice an increase in contrast and noise in images captured at these elevated resolutions.

The presence of high ISO noise can be attributed to the amplification required to enhance the sensor's sensitivity. Although elevated ISOs do extract details from dimly lit regions, they also generate noise by arbitrarily amplifying non-signal information. The High ISO NR option can be located within the Photo Shooting menu. From there, you have the ability to choose between High, Normal, or Low noise reduction, or disable the feature entirely. Noise reduction has the tendency to diminish the image's detail and soften its pixelated appearance; therefore, if you are prepared to tolerate a small amount of noise in exchange for more information, you may wish to disable the feature.

Additionally, extended exposure times result in a comparable chaotic phenomenon, allowing for a greater number of photons to reach the sensor and thereby enhancing the ability to capture images in low-light conditions. However, extended exposures also increase the probability that some pixels will detect illusory photons at random. This is frequently the case because as an imager remains "hot," its temperature rises, which can be misinterpreted as heat rather than photons. An additional type of noise exists to which CMOS sensors, such as those employed in the Z8, will be particularly vulnerable. There are millions of individual amplifiers and A/D converters in CMOS imagers, all of which operate in concert. Due to the fact that these circuits may not consistently operate in an identical manner, they have the potential to introduce fixed-pattern noise into the image data. Thankfully, the electronics wizards at Nikon have performed admirably in reducing noise from all sources within the camera.

Nevertheless, you may still wish to utilize the long exposure noise reduction option, which can be enabled via Long Exp. By accessing the Photo Shooting menu, one can enable or disable the NR feature. This form of noise reduction entails the camera capturing an additional, empty exposure and subsequently comparing the stochastic pixels present in that image to the one that was just captured. Pixels that align in both images concurrently constitute noise and may be effectively omitted. Dark frame subtraction, a noise reduction technique that effectively doubles the exposure time, is only applied to photographs with durations exceeding one second. As a result of noise reduction, the image may lose some detail, as some image information may be lost in the process. Consequently, this feature should be utilized sparingly. Additionally, a limited degree of noise reduction can be achieved with Photoshop and your preferred RAW converter when converting RAW files to another format; an industrial-strength product such as Noise Ninja (www.picturecode.com) can be utilized to eliminate noise from captured images after they have been developed.

ABOUT THE Z8 BRACKETING

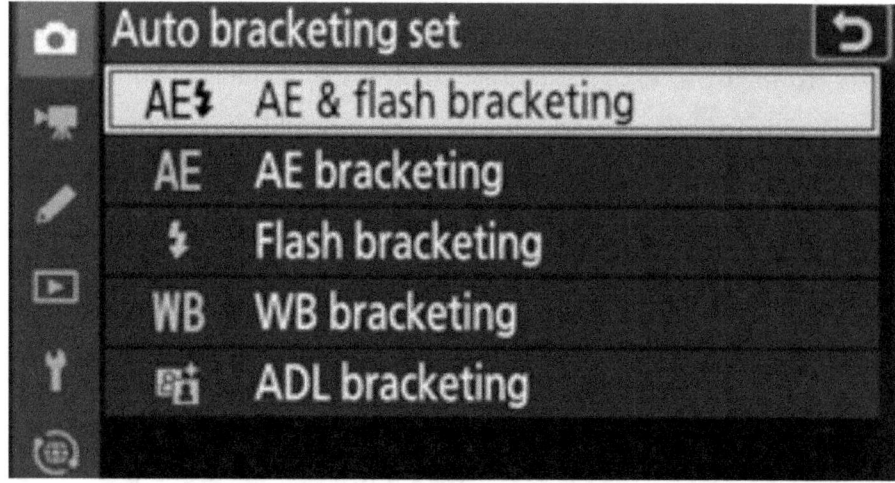

By shooting multiple consecutive exposures with varying settings, bracketing increases the probability that one will be precisely accurate. To generate a series of photographs featuring marginally distinct white balances or exposures with the expectation that one of the exposures will be "better" from a creative perspective, bracketing can also be utilized. Bracketing can provide, for instance, a standard exposure for a backlit subject, a "underexposed" exposure that generates a silhouette effect, and an "overexposed" exposure that generates an additional appearance.

In addition to bracketing exposures with greater precision, the Z8 can also bracket white balance and active D-lighting. Although WB bracketing is occasionally employed when color accuracy is critical, auto exposure bracketing is significantly more prevalent. Upon activation of this function, the camera executes a sequence of consecutive images: commencing with the predetermined "correct"

100

exposure, followed by shots with a decreasing exposure, and concluding with shots increasing the exposure by a desired increment of +3/–3 stops. As bracketed exposures are created in S mode, the aperture will change while the shutter speed varies in A mode. Although configuring auto exposure bracketing parameters is more difficult than it ought to be, the process can be simplified by following these steps:

1. Select bracketing type: To begin, navigate to the Auto Bracketing entry in the Photo Shooting menu and select the desired bracketing type using Auto Bracketing Set. ADL bracketing, auto exposure and flash, flash only, white balance only, and auto exposure and flash are all options. You can define the bracketing process using Custom Setting e6 if they intend to photograph in Manual exposure mode. There, you can select between flash and shutter speed, aperture and flash and shutter speed, flash and aperture, or flash only. ADL bracketing and white balance are not accessible in manual exposure mode.

2. Select bracketing order: Custom Setting e7 allows for the selection of bracket orders as follows: MTR > Under > Over or Under > MTR > Over.

3. Select number of bracketed exposures: To determine the quantity of bracketed exposures, navigate to the Auto Bracketing entry in the Photo Shooting menu and select Number of Shots. From there, use the touch screen or the left/right buttons of the multi selector to determine the number of shots with underexposure (minus) or overexposure (plus)

in the sequence: press left to disable bracketing at zero, press right to select –2, +2, –3, or +3. To specify 3-, 5-, 7-, or 9-shot bracket sets centered on the metered exposure, press the appropriate button.

4. Select bracket increment: Subsequently, select Increment and select the exposure increment using the touch screen, left/right buttons, 1/3, 2/3, 1, 2, or 3 EV. Please be advised that if you choose an increment of 2 EV or 3 EV, the designated number of photos in the bracketed set in Step 3 is restricted to 5. In Step 3, if you selected seven or nine photos, the camera will convert the setting to five photographs automatically.

5. Choose bracket increment: While shooting, the camera will adjust the exposure, flash level, and white balance for each individual image in the sequence specified in Custom Setting e7, contingent upon the bracketing "program" that you have chosen. You must press the shutter release button the specified number of times for each exposure in your bracketed burst in Single-frame mode.

6. Deactivate bracketing: Once the bracketing process is complete, navigate back to the Auto Bracketing entry and modify the Number of Shots to 0. This will prevent the BKT indicator from being displayed, as the setting will remain active even after the camera is powered off and powered back on.

After establishing the desired type of bracketing, capturing a series of bracketed exposures is straightforward. To commence the exposure of a set while bracketing is active, simply select the Bracketing Burst icon. (To designate the Bracketing Burst behavior to a button, utilize Custom Setting f2.) For each instance in which the shutter release trigger is tapped once, the entire set will be captured.

White Balance Bracketing

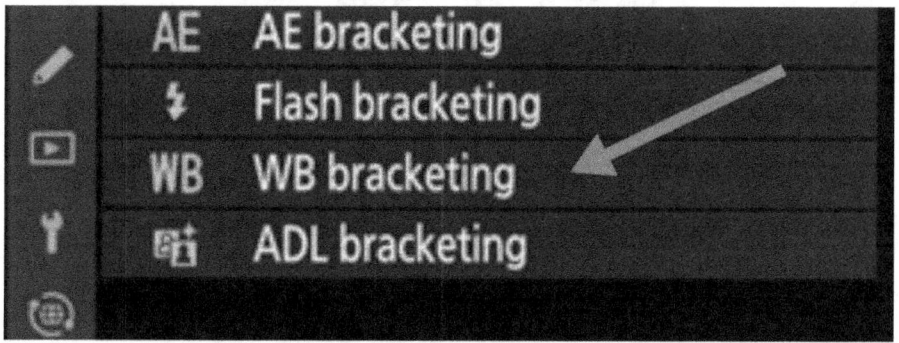

The camera does not capture three distinct exposures when white balance bracketing is selected; even if a bracketing burst button is defined, only one picture will be captured. There is no necessity upon reflection. RAW exposure is captured first, irrespective of the camera's mode setting (JPEG, RAW, or RAW+JPEG). After selecting JPEG-only mode, the camera applies the specified settings to convert the initial RAW exposure to JPEG format, and subsequently deletes the RAW data. When in RAW mode, the camera generates a Basic JPEG rendition of the image, which is embedded as a thumbnail in the RAW file, in addition to storing the RAW data as a NEF file. When you examine your photographs on the back-panel LCD monitor, that thumbnail is what you see; you never see the RAW file in its entirety until you import it into an image editor. When presenting a RAW image, the embedded JPEG file may also be utilized by your computer. In conclusion, the NEF RAW file (containing its own embedded JPEG image) and a distinct JPEG file of the quality level you designate (Fine, Normal, or Basic) are produced when you save in RAW+JPEG format.

As the initially captured RAW file comprises all digital information acquired during exposure, white balance bracketing reduces the number of images the camera needs to capture to one. Subsequently, a JPEG file is generated at each of the specified white balance settings. You receive two or three JPEG files of the specified quality level, bracketed as you specify, with a single click. Quite effective. As you might expect, WB bracketing is only applied to JPEG files; RAW and RAW+JPEG settings do not permit the specification of WB bracketing. RAW files are consistently preserved in their original state and undergo a conversion process in the image editor that corresponds to the white balance settings selected in the camera, assuming no adjustments are made to the white balance during importation.

In contrast to exposure bracketing, which results in JPEG files that differ by f stops, white balance bracketing utilizes micro reciprocal degrees () to specify color temperature. Aside from the fact that WB bracketing modifies the color temperature of your images by 5 mireds for each picture captured in the bracket set, there is really no need to comprehend mireds. Only adjustments are implemented in the amber-blue spectrum; the green-magenta color bias remains unaffected by bracketing. To enable White Balance bracketing, simply execute the subsequent procedures:

1. JPEG Only: Within the Photo Shooting menu, ensure that the Image Quality entry is set to JPEG-only.

2. Specify WB Bracketing: As your bracketing configuration, select WB Bracketing from the Auto Bracketing entry in the Photo Shooting menu.

3. Choose number of shots: After selecting WB Bracketing on the Auto Bracketing interface, navigate to Number of Shots and enter the desired number of bracketed exposures. You have two distinct options:

- By utilizing the right directional button and selecting from zero to nine, the camera will execute the designated quantity of shots in both the amber and blue directions, with an even distribution of shots on either side of the zero point on the amber-blue scale. For example, selecting 5 as the number of bullets will result in the sequence comprising one neutral shot and two shots that are biased by 5 and 10 mireds in the direction of amber and blue, respectively. Bracketing is deactivated when the number of images is set to zero, the same applies to exposure bracketing.

- By utilizing the left directional button, one can choose between two and three images with an A3 or B2, A2, B3, or blue bias imposed on the camera. B3 would, for instance, consist of projectiles with biases of 5, 10, and 15 mireds exclusively in the blue direction.

ADL Bracketing

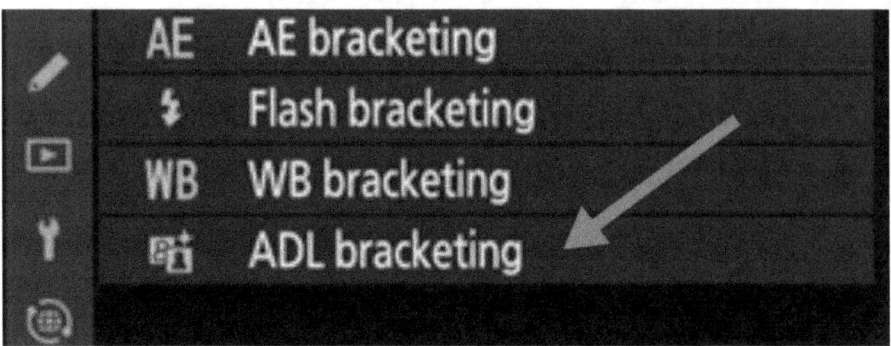

To activate Active D-Lighting bracketing, select it from the Auto Bracketing Set menu entry in the Photo Shooting menu and enter the desired number and quantity of photos. Similar to exposure bracketing, a burst can be initiated with a single stroke of the shutter release button if a Bracketing Burst button has been defined. Settable strikes are limited to the following:

1. 0 (Number of shots): Disables active D-lighting bracketing. Only bracketing is deactivated. In the Shooting menu, enabling basic Active D-Lighting will result in the application of the specified quantity of ADL to each shot (Auto, Extra High, High, Normal, or Low).

2. 2 (Number of shots): One photo will be taken with the ADL (control, so to speak) turned off, and the other will be taken at the setting you specify. Down, locate the Amount box. Off/Auto (Auto ADL + No ADL), Off/Extra High, Off/High, Off/Normal, and Off/Low are all options.

3. 3–5 (Number of shots): Choose from three, four, or five shots. One will be set to Off (ADL disabled), while the remaining ones will be provided at the values specified in the Amount field. (The ADL specifications cannot be modified in the Amount box when three, four, or five photos are recorded.)

-   3 shots: Off, Normal, and Low.

-   4 shots: zero, plus, standard, and high.

-   5 shots: Off, Low, Normal, High, and Extra High.

Similar to how you should disable WB, exposure, and flash bracketing, ensure that ADL bracketing is turned off when not in use. It is automatically activated during each photograph taken until it is deactivated.

WORKING WITH HDR

For instance, if you wish to capture an outdoor scene through a brilliant window in a dimly illuminated room. The ideal exposure for the interior would be approximately 1/60 second at f/2.8 and ISO 200, whereas the exterior scene would likely demand f/11 at 1/400 second. This significantly exceeds the dynamic range of any digital camera, including the z8 (approximately 7 f/stops or 7 EV step difference).

Until sensors acquire significantly greater dynamic ranges, which may not be as distant in the future as we currently believe, advanced techniques such as HDR photography and Active D-Lighting will continue to be fundamental tools. You can create HDR exposures in-camera with the z8 or shoot HDR the traditional way—with distinct bracketed exposures that are merged in an image-editing application such as Photomatix or Adobe's Merge to HDR feature. Listed below are the ways to utilize HDR:

Auto HDR

Even though the in-camera HDR function is uncomplicated and lacks flexibility, it is remarkably effective at producing images with a high dynamic range. It is also extraordinarily user-friendly. While it solely merges two images into a solitary HDR photograph, it is comparable to the manual HDR method in certain respects. As an illustration, it permits the specification of a three-stop/EV exposure differential between the two photos, identical to the process followed when capturing bracketed exposures.

It is worth noting that capturing detail in both shadows and highlights within a single image using digital sensors can be challenging due to the limited dynamic range of the sensor, which comprises the number of tones. The resolution, specifically in this instance, was to utilize the Auto HDR function of the camera to merge the two exposures into a single image.

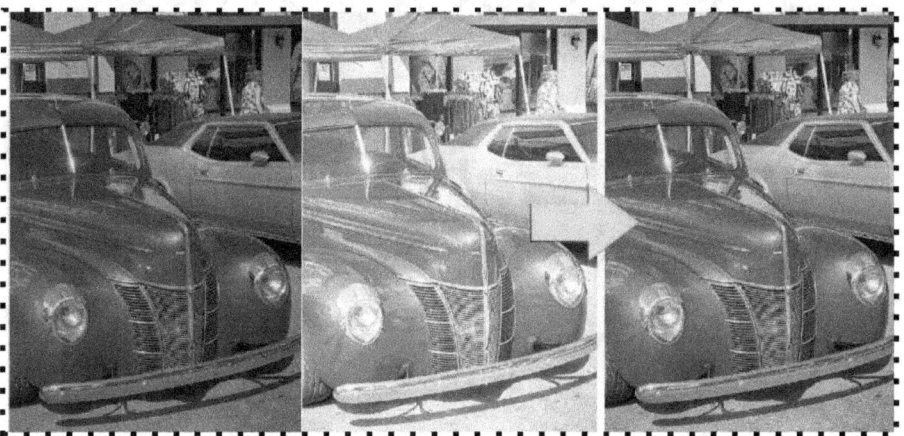

The image above depicts a potential appearance of the two photos merged by the HDR function. A three-stop disparity exists between the image at the left, which is underexposed, and the image in the center, which is overexposed. The in-camera HDR processing can combine the two to produce an image with a significantly greater spectrum of tones, similar to the one displayed on the right.

To utilize the HDR function, simply adhere to these steps. When RAW or RAW+JPEG is selected, the function is inoperable. Additionally, it is not compatible with bracketing functions, multiple exposure, or time-lapse photography.

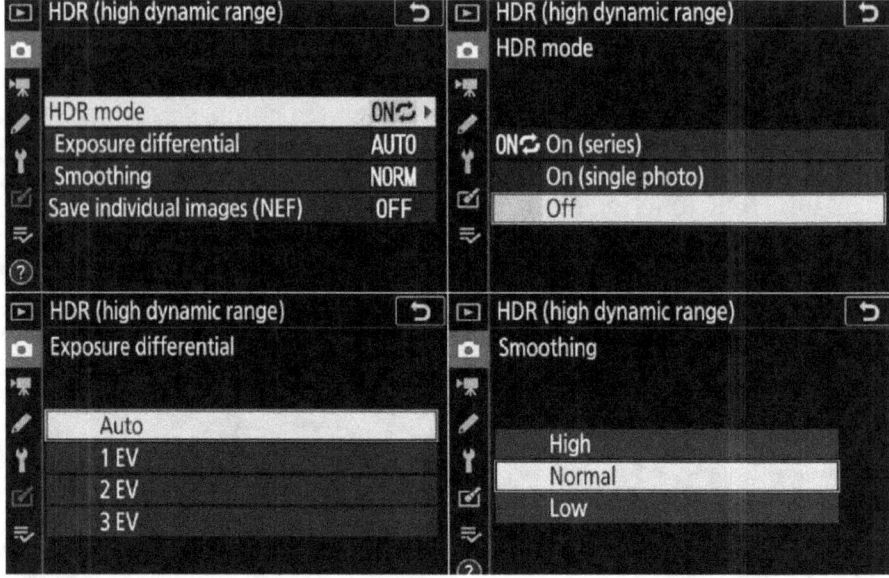

1. Enable the Menu: By selecting the Photo Shooting menu (represented by a camera icon), press the MENU button.

2. Scroll down to HDR and press the multi-selector button on the right. Four options—HDR Mode, Exposure Differential, Smoothing, and Save Individual Images, will be presented on a subsequent screen.

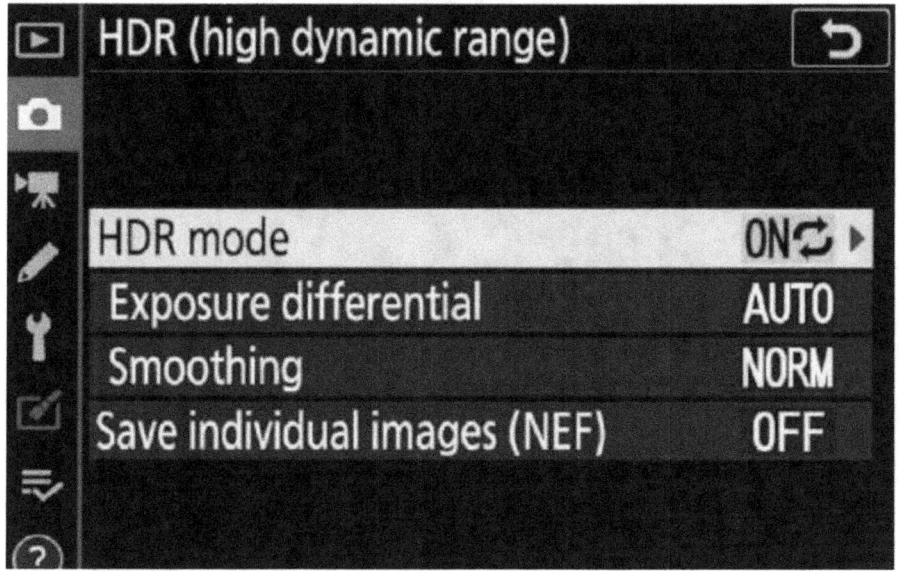

3. To activate HDR, select HDR Mode, hold the right button, and then choose On (single photo) or On (series) to capture multiple HDR images consecutively or a single HDR image, respectively, before turning off the feature. Select OFF to deactivate the function. Select OK to confirm your choice.

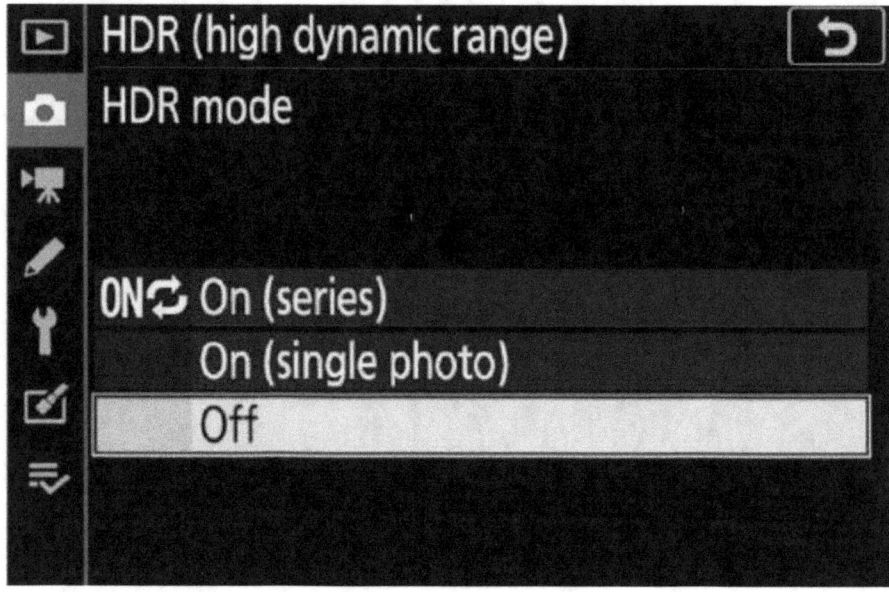

4. Set amount: Select Exposure Differential, then press the right button and select Auto, 1 EV, 2 EV, or 3 EV (the camera determines the contrast ratio of the scene and applies the appropriate differential). Auto is an excellent option for preliminary experiments. Alternately, assign a greater EV strength to subjects with greater contrast and a lesser value to subjects with reduced contrast. Select OK to verify your choice.

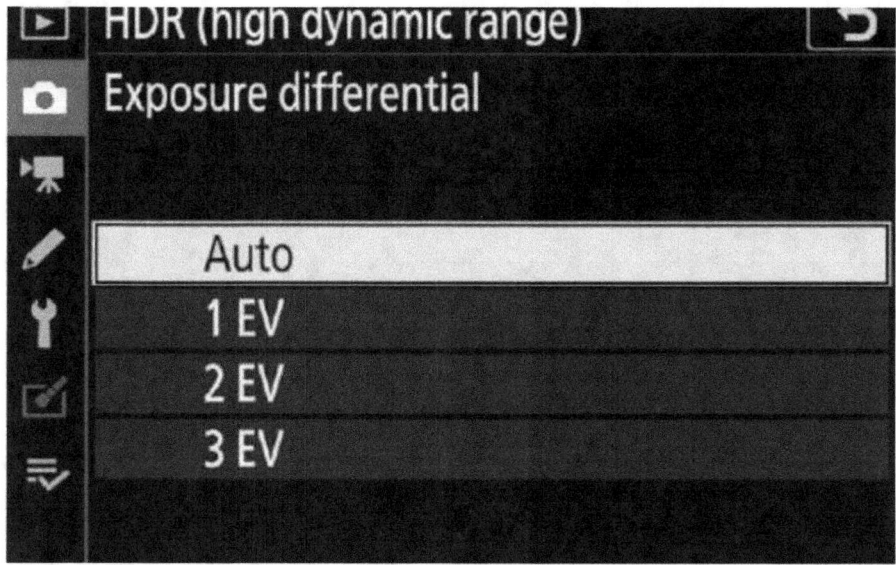

5. Choose smoothing: Smoothing is recommended, as HDR can result in haloing around the perimeters of regions in an image. By selecting from the Normal, Low, or High Smoothing values, the effect can be modified.

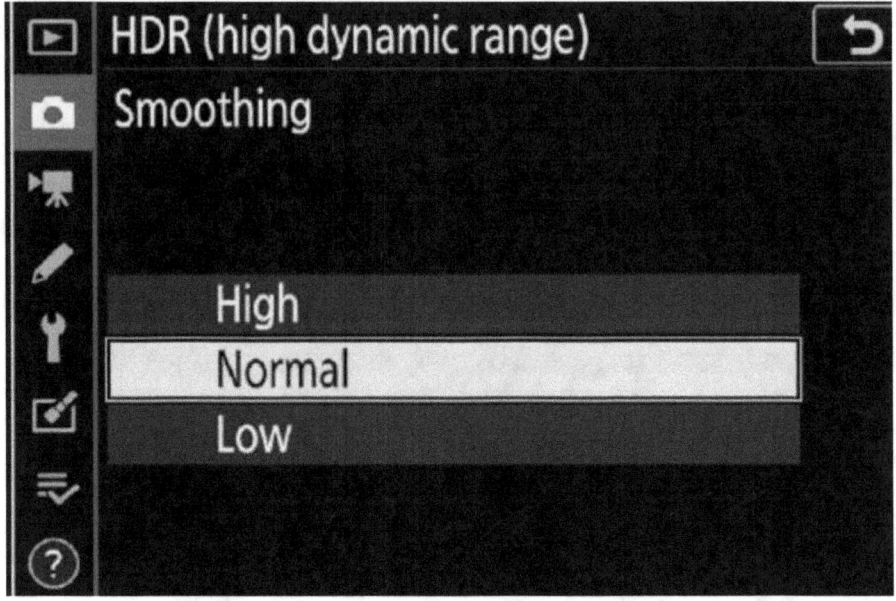

6. Save Individual Images (optional): While the camera will automatically combine two images into an HDR picture, the individual images are not deleted. If Save Individual Images (NEF) is enabled, a Large RAW rendition of each captured image will be stored in the camera, irrespective of whether RAW or Large image quality/size has been selected. The intermediate images will be accessible for modification or refinement on your personal computer.

7. Configure Aperture-Priority mode: You should adjust exposure by adjusting the f/stop as opposed to the aperture, so that the depth-of-field remains constant across all shots.

8. Finally take your shot: Incorporate aperture priority mode into your camera. While HDR can be captured unaided, optimal results are achieved when the camera is tripod-mounted and

the subject matter exhibits does not move that much. It should be noted that due to the camera's attempt to align photos, even minimal camera movement will result in the cropping of certain portions of the images at the margins. It is advisable to utilize a tripod when employing Auto HDR, despite its satisfactory performance when used handheld.

Bracketing and Merge to HDR

HDR can also be captured manually, independent of the HDR mode on the camera. Conversely, individual images can be captured by employing either the manual bracketing or automatic bracketing protocols. When utilizing Merge to HDR Pro, multiple images are captured, with some serving as exposure controls for shadows, midtones, and highlights, respectively. You can choose the precise quantity of images to merge. Then, combine all of the images into a single HDR image using the Merge to HDR Pro command, which incorporates the well-exposed portions of each version. Aside from exposure, the images should be as identical as feasible. Consequently, it is prudent to affix the camera to a tripod, employ a remote release device such as the MC-DC2, and capture each exposure simultaneously. Follow these instructions precisely:

1. Set up the camera: Establish the camera atop a tripod.

2. Configure the camera to shoot bracketed bursts at 2 or 3 EV increments.

3. Select an f-stop: Configure the camera to Aperture-priority mode and choose an aperture that will yield an accurate

exposure for the sequence of manually bracketed images at the initial settings.

4. Select manual focus: To prevent focus fluctuations between photos, configure the camera to manual focus and aim the subject with care.

5. Opt for RAW exposures: Configure the camera to capture RAW files for images with the greatest possible spectrum of tones.

6. Utilize the bracketed set: Capture the series of bracketed exposures by pressing the button on the remote, pressing the shutter release with caution, or using the self-timer.

7. Proceed with the subsequent Merge to HDR Pro instructions that will pop up next.

TROUBLESHOOTING PROBLEMS ON THE Z8

Every device encounters at least one malfunction, and the Nikon Z8 is not an exception. The following are frequent difficulties encountered when troubleshooting the Nikon Z8:

The Z8 cannot be powered on.

If you are unable to power on your Nikon Z8 camera despite your attempts, consider the following:

1. Verify that the battery is being charged and that it is properly positioned.

2. Scrutinize the battery connections, ensure that they are devoid of any debris.

3. Try to power on the camera by using a distinct brand of battery.

4. Contacting Nikon's customer support or visiting an authorized repair facility is advised if the camera still refuses to power on.

Autofocus Difficulties

Autofocus malfunctions can significantly impair the functionality of your camera. If one is encountering difficulties with autofocus, the following solutions should be attempted:

1. Verify that the lens's autofocus mechanism is in the "AF" (autofocus) position by examining its location.

2. Navigate to the camera's menu and examine the focus mode settings to ensure that the desired autofocus mode (such as Single AF or Continuous AF) is selected.

3. After wiping the lens contacts clear, ensure that they are affixed securely to the camera body.

4. Ensure that the firmware on your camera is current, as focusing capabilities are frequently enhanced in newer software versions.

5. Should the problem persist, send the camera and lens to an authorized service facility for calibration or repair.

Image Quality Issues

Should you observe a reduction in the quality of the images or encounter any other complications related to the images, consider the subsequent troubleshooting measures:

1. Ensure that the parameters on your camera, including the ISO, white balance, and image controls, are appropriate for the circumstances under which you will be photographing.

2. Utilize a sensor cleansing device designed specifically for your camera model in order to cleanse the image sensor.

3. Conduct an exhaustive inspection of the lens in order to identify any potential defects such as smudges, grime, or blemishes that could undermine the quality of the image. A

microfibre cloth or a lens cleaning solution may be utilized to wipe the lens.

4. Consistently ensure that the firmware of the camera is updated to the most recent, as Nikon frequently releases firmware updates to address various issues and improve image quality.

5. Should you continue to encounter challenges regarding the quality of your images, it is advisable to contact Nikon's customer service or visit an authorized service facility for assistance.

Error Messages

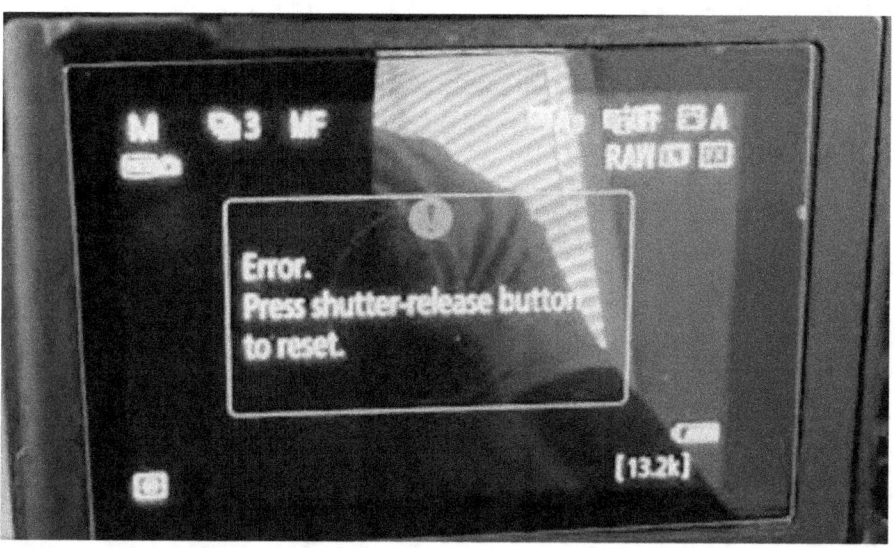

Error messages may be construed to signify a multitude of camera-related complications. A list of common error messages and their respective potential resolutions is provided below:

1. Message "Err": Frequently, this error message signifies a potential malfunction of the camera. One possible solution is to remove and reinstall the battery while ensuring that it is fully charged. You should immediately contact Nikon's customer service if the issue persists.

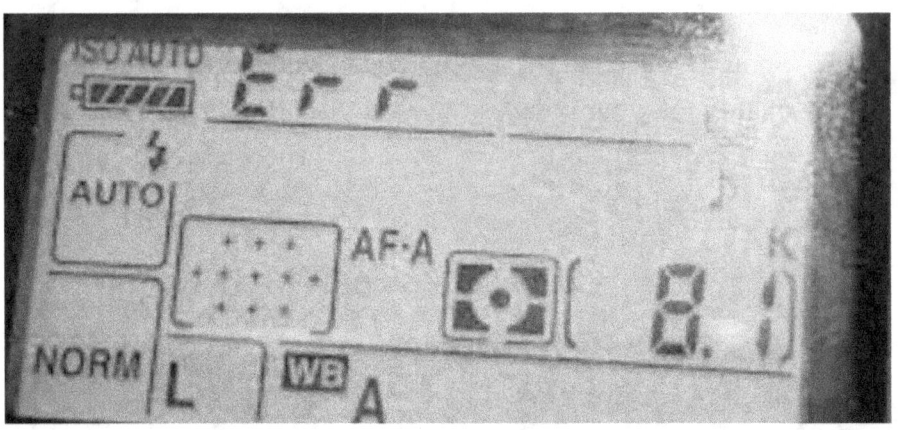

2. If the "Card is full" or "Card cannot be read" message appears: Verify that the memory card has been inserted into the camera properly. If the problem persists, replace the memory card or perform a card formatting operation on the one that is presently in use (note that card formatting erases all data stored on the card).

3. If the message "Lens not attached" appears: Verify that the lens is affixed to the camera body securely. Remove the lens and reattach it, this time ensure that it snaps into position.

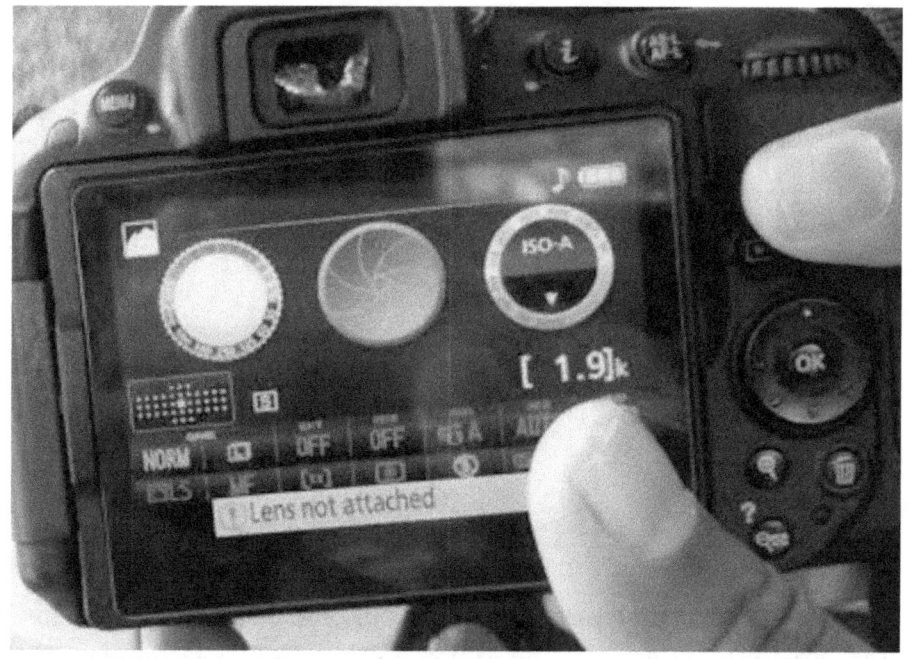

Connectivity Problems

Follow these steps if you are experiencing issues connecting your Nikon Z8 to other devices or if the camera's wireless functionality is malfunctioning:

1. Ensure that the Wi-Fi and Bluetooth configurations are properly enabled and properly configured on the camera.

2. Confirm that the device to which you are trying to connect your camera satisfies the requisite protocols and specifications for the execution of a compatibility test between the two devices.

3. Ensure that the firmware of the camera is fully updated to the most recent version, as software updates frequently include connection enhancements.

4. Try to get specific instructions regarding the connection of Wi-Fi or the resolution of connectivity issues from the camera user manual.

5. If the problem persists, please contact Nikon's customer support for further assistance or consult an authorized service facility.

Overheating

It is possible that prolonged use of the Nikon Z8 camera could cause it to overheat, in which case it will issue an overheating warning and its performance will be negatively impacted. Try one of the solutions listed below to alleviate this issue:

1. It is best to minimize the use of the camera in atmospheres that are excessively heated or in direct sunlight.

2. Deactivate any unnecessary camera functions, including picture preview, long exposure noise reduction, and continuous photography, in order to reduce the camera's workload.

3. Before resuming use, allow the camera to fully get cool by deactivating it and removing the battery for a brief interval.

4. It is advisable to utilize an external fan or alternative cooling apparatus during extended photography sessions in order to augment the ventilation surrounding the camera.

Battery Drain

In the event that the battery life of your Nikon Z8 diminishes quickly, proceed with the subsequent procedures:

1. It is imperative to utilize an authentic Nikon battery and charger. Using a counterfeit or incompatible battery with your camera could hasten the depletion of its power supply.

2. Conduct an exhaustive search for any functions or settings that consume a considerable quantity of power, such as continuous focusing or frequent use of the LCD screen.

3. Modify the camera menu options for the auto power-off function in order to reduce the duration of the camera's inactive state.

4. Verify that the battery contacts are in excellent working order and are free of any debris or corrosion.

5. Try replacing the battery if the issue with its depletion persists, or contact Nikon's customer service for further assistance.

SD Cards Problems

Experiencing difficulties with your SD cards may result in data loss, write errors, or other complications. Do the following actions to resolve these problems:

1. It is pertinent to verify that the SD card being utilized is compatible and has been formatted accurately.

2. To ensure optimal functionality and compatibility, the SD card should be formatted immediately via the camera. It is important to note, however, that formatting the card will result in the complete deletion of any data contained on it. Therefore, prior to formatting, ensure that any important files have been backed up.

3. In the event that the camera presents an error message associated with the SD card, it is advisable to insert the card into a computer and employ disk repair or formatting software to address any potential file system malfunctions. In the absence of an SD card-related error message, the camera might be corrupted.

4. To mitigate the likelihood of data corruption or other complications associated with the card, it is advisable to consider purchasing SD cards manufactured by reputable companies that exhibit superior quality.

5. If the problem persists or the SD card is damaged tangibly, replace it with a different card or contact Nikon customer service for further assistance.

Firmware or Software Problems

Follow the steps below to address these kind of problems:

1. Please visit the official Nikon website in order to identify any firmware updates that may be available. If you update the firmware, there is a likelihood that the camera's overall performance will be enhanced.

2. Alternatively, you can factory reset the camera; In order to restore the camera to its initial factory state and erase all settings, adhere to the factory reset steps specified in the user manual. This might aid in the resolution of issues or challenges associated with the software's configuration.

3. Should you encounter difficulties with specific functions or settings of the camera, such as menu navigation or button responsiveness, consult the Nikon customer support service or visit an authorized service center for additional assistance.

www.ingramcontent.com/pod-product-compliance
Lightning Source LLC
Chambersburg PA
CBHW071050290526
45795CB00004B/1408